CHRISTIANITY
ITS ECONOMY AND WAY OF LIFE

D1871073

Owing to the antiquity and rarity of this book, certain pages are regrettably absent, and readability is compromised due to the blurring of the original text. If you possess any insights regarding the availability of these missing sections, kindly inform us. Your assistance is crucial in ensuring the completion of this significant work for the benefit of future generations.

CHRISTIANITY
ITS ECONOMY AND WAY OF LIFE

BY

J. C. KUMARAPPA

GYAN

Published by

GYAN

Gyan Publishing House
5, Ansari Road
Daryaganj, New Delhi-110002
Phone: 011-47034999, 9811692060
E-mail: books@gyanbooks.com

Distribution Network
gyanbooks.com
India, USA, Canada, UK, Australia

© Publisher

All rights reserved. No part of this work may be reproduced, stored, adapted, or transmitted in any form or by any means, electronic, mechanical, photocopying, micro-filming, recording or otherwise, or translated in any language, without the prior written permission of the copyright owner and the publisher.

ISBN: 978-93-6208-710-2 (PB)
First Published, 1945

2nd Impression 2024

Printed at: Gyan Press, Delhi.

The book is sold subject to the condition that it shall not, by way of trade or otherwise, be lent, resold, hired out, or otherwise circulated without the prior publisher's written consent.

CHRISTIANITY ITS ECONOMY AND WAY OF LIFE
Author: J. C. KUMARAPPA

CHRISTIANITY
ITS ECONOMY AND WAY OF LIFE

BY

J. C. KUMARAPPA

PREFACE

This booklet is a collection of addresses delivered on various occasions to Christian audiences with the exception of "The Religion of Jesus" which was read at the Parliament of Religions. It is hoped that the non-Christian reader will find no difficulty in following the context of Biblical quotations.

The background and date of each chapter are stated under the caption with the hope that the repetitions unavoidable in such a compilation as this will only serve to add further light and emphasis on the principles dealt with and will not weary the reader.

Some of the chapters were salvaged from summaries and reports of the speeches. Hence they naturally present certain difficulties consequent on overcondensation but we trust that in spite of this the message stands out clearly.

Though the manuscript was ready for the printers in November 1942, the publication was delayed owing to various unavoidable circumstances.

While this volume presents a critical approach to the practice of the church, a rethinking of the teachings of Jesus has been attempted in a companion volume entitled "The Practice and Precepts of Jesus".

Maganwadi, Wardha J. C. KUMARAPPA
25 June, 1945

CONTENTS

Part I

CORRECTION : In chapter heading of chapter II read 'worship' for 'workship'.

For thus saith the Lord of hosts, the God of Israel; Let not your prophets and your diviners, that be in the midst of you, deceive you, neither hearken to your dreams which ye cause to be dreamed.

For they prophesy falsely unto you in my name: I have not sent them, saith the Lord.

Jer. : XXIX 8-9.

Beware lest any man spoil you through philosophy and vain deceit, after the tradition of men, after the rudiments of the world, and not after Christ.

Col. : II 8

But I fear, lest by any means, as the serpent beguiled eve through his subtility, so your minds should be corrupted from the simplicity that is in Christ. II Cor. : XI 3

. . . . but there be some that trouble you, and would pervert the gospel of Christ.

But though we, or an angel from heaven, preach any other gospel unto you . . . . let him be accursed. Gal. : I 7-8

CHRISTIANITY
ITS ECONOMY AND WAY OF LIFE

I

THE ECONOMY OF THE CROSS

(*Being a summary of three addresses delivered at the Mid-India Conference of Christian Students at Nagpur, the 5th - 7th November 1942.*)

I trust you do not expect to listen to a detailed programme of reconstruction as is usually set out in schemes by government and other bodies giving a cut and dry list of items that can be carried out along with picturesque descriptions of such things as sanitary devices, sinking and cleaning of wells, utilization of waste, hygienic precautions to be taken etc. These we must needs have, but much more important is the spirit of approach. If we have the right attitude we shall be able to lay out an effective programme for ourselves. Our mission should not be merely ameliorative but should be directed towards a definite end, if we call ourselves Christians, towards fulfilling the mission of Jesus who came that "they might have life and that they might have it more abundantly". With this view in mind I shall strive to place before you the principles of Jesus to be applied in economic reconstruction. Once we grasp these fundamentals all other details will naturally fit into their right places and settings in the picture.

We may group, in a general way, the principles followed in economic organizations or systems under two heads :- 1. those which are transient and 2. those which are permanent. And the systems based on these principles we may speak of as Economy of Transience and Economy of Permanence.

ECONOMY OF TRANSIENCE

It is customary to designate the different types of systems taking into consideration the material factors operating in each. But as we regard human factors much more vital we shall attempt to evaluate the different types from the kind of reaction each system produces in man in relation to his upward career from the brute level. In the main we may classify the many forms of economy followed in the past under these categories. 1. Economy of Predation, 2. Economy of Enterprise, 3. Economy of Gregarianism.

Economy of Predation — In the animal kingdom generally the system which prevails, and is dominant, is the Economy of Predation. Its main characteristic is that consumption takes place without corresponding production. Monkeys do not plant fruit trees, water and nurture them and then eat their fruit. They just pluck and eat. Similarly, tigers do not organize cattle breeding farms. They kill and devour. In the same way, man in his nomadic stages hunted and fished. He reaped where he sowed not and gathered where he strawed not. This is the most rudimentary form of economic activity. It is purely selfish or 'animalish'. The desire to get something for nothing is degrading to man and reduces him to the brute level. Such activities contribute nothing to the development of the higher nature in man. Such an economy is based on rights and recognizes no duties towards one's neighbours. The age old question "Am I my brother's keeper?" reverberates throughout this world as the prevailing criterion, and the answer still is in the negative, and serves as the criterion of individual and international action, based on the high sounding philosoply of laissez-faire. Protection against physical death is the lodestar of existence. Unabated greed propels man to exploit his fellows to supply his insatiable artificial wants. Man lives and dies like a dog.

When such a system is coupled with political power it leads to imperialism which Tagore characterizes as the modern form of cannibalism. The latest forms of this type of economy attempt to control the lives of other nations, countries and ocean routes, and replace the cruder form of slave economy. This economy goes counter to Jesus' teaching "love thy neighbour as thyself". Hence it is of no value to us.

Economy of Enterprise — The next stage in the upward journey of man is the Economy of Enterprise. In the animal kingdom beavers, bees, ants etc., also follow this economy to an extent. In this system something is contributed by the consumer towards production before consumption takes place. This effort cultivates forethought. The talents man is endowed with are used to the fullest extent. The reaction is beneficial to the growth of man's faculties but his guiding principle is still centred in the well being of the self.

The copy book maxim "Every man for himself and the devil take the hindermost" prevails.

By dint of his intellect man impresses into his service the great forces of nature. His life consists in the abundance of things he possesses. Our souls may be required of us this night; then whose shall these things be which we have provided after much thought and labour? We have to get beyond this economy and learn that life is more than meat and the body more than raiment.

In this economy we find the capitalist and the industrialist bound down to the earth and the golden calf installed on a high pedestal. There is little recognition of the fact that "As for man, his days are as grass; as a flower of the field so he flourisheth. For the wind passeth over it and it is gone and the place thereof shall know it no more".

Jesus commands "Sell all thou hast and give to the poor." This calls us to use all our faculties for the benefit of those less richly endowed than we are. Will the Christian youth turn away from this ideal saying that they need all they can make to keep up their high standard of living? Will they use their faculties to command that stones be made bread for their own consumption and enjoyment, or will they realize themselves by dedicating their talents and prossessions to the service of the masses?

Economy of Gregarianism :—Some species of animals like wolves, elephants etc., lead group lives for hunting in packs or for safety in herding together. Similarly, certain groups of men protect themselves by projecting their interests beyond themselves and, adoring tribal leaders or ancestors, group together to act and live for a common purpose. This stage is less self-centred than the former two but has its great limitations. There is a rising consciousness of duty to sink his personal interest for the common good. Here is the dawn of neighbourliness and idealism but it is not yet universal.

Communism visualizes such an extension of life, but fails to appreciate that man does not live by bread alone. What shall it profit a man if he gains the whole world and loses his own soul? Ignoring the truth of this statement, it gives more consideration to material values rather than to the spiritual. Hence this method with the background of predation and enterprise leads to Fascism and Nazism where the State is enthroned and becomes the be-all and the end-all of existence, and the interests of the individual are sacrificed to those of the State. The slogan "My country, right or wrong" draws the blind and slavish loyalty of the people. We thus transfer the allegiance, devotion and worship we owe to God to a man-made organization contrary to the command "Thou shalt worship the Lord thy God and Him only shalt thou serve".

Under all these three forms within the Economy of Transience man is not far removed from the dumb animals and though his methods may be more refined yet he does not manifest any qualities peculiarly his own. At the highest, he can but view himself as the Lord of Creation. All these activities are of the earth, earthy. Hence their consequences are limited by space and time. They are motivated by lower passions rather than by a set purpose. Violence characterizes everyone of them and they are subject to regulation by external discipline. With all the glamour of life under what is termed "Western civilization" introduced by the predatory British imperialism, by the enterprising American industrialism, and by the drive of the Russian and German gregarianism, we do not even approach the realities of man's destiny but still remain just "dumb driven cattle" at best.

In what way is the Christian youth different from those materialists "for after all these things do the gentiles seek". Has Jesus anything better to offer? Yes. He points us to the Economy of Permanence when He says "Seek ye first the Kingdom of God, and His righteousness and all these things shall be added unto you".

ECONOMY OF PERMANENCE

In the Economy of Transience man sees himself as the central figure in the universe. When he has evolved sufficiently high spiritually he comes to the realizations that he is less than dust and that his body is but a temporary abode and is a machine subject to heavy depreciation. It is then and then alone that he begins to visualize God's creation in true perspective. He becomes aware of his higher self and distinguishes the glory of the celestial body from the fleeting pleasures ot this terrestrial body. Now he falls in line with the universal scheme of his Creator and sows a natural body to put on immortality. The truth in the statement of Jesus — "whosoever will save his life shall lose it; but whosoever shall lose his life for my sake and the

Gospel's the same shall find life eternal" — dawns on him and he finds "death is swallowed up in victory".

This then is the basic principle which should govern the life of the Christian youth. This is the one thing needful. Once we accept this code all material values will yield place to cultural standards. Selfishness and greed will no longer ride on our backs nor shall we be slaves to any predatory power. Our actions will be motivated by a well defined purpose in life and will not be tossed about on the billows of desire. Multiplicity of wants cannot dominate and rule our lives reducing us to the serfdom of material goods. On the contrary, our enterprise will bear fruit a thousand-fold. We shall rise above petty nationalism and qualify for the citizenship of the Kingdom of God. There shall be neither Greek nor Jew, circumcision nor uncircumcision, barbarian nor Scythian, bond nor free. We shall be distinguished from the brutes in that our actions will not be based on might and rights but on duties and responsibilities, and our work will be an abiding prayer and worship. Our life will not be towed along the economic plans of a complex life laid out by interested industrialists. We shall steer our own simple lives by self-control and discipline. Then alone shall we be able to forsake mammon and worship God in truth and in spirit, as the good Samaritan did, by serving the needy around us in a spirit of self-abnegation. Jesus directs: "Heal the sick, cleanse the lepers, freely ye have received, freely give. Provide neither gold, nor silver, nor brass in your purses, nor scrip for your journey, neither two coats, neither shoes, nor yet staves: for the workman is worthy of his meat".

The infusion of these ideals into economics is essential if we aim at securing for the people a life of peace and plenty. The principles involved being based on fundamentals will remain for all time and will not have to be varied according to the exigencies of the situation.

Democracy and the State—Every individual, if he is self-disciplined and free, represents sovereign power. In the life of any group certain common functions have to be performed in the interests of all. Such are best carried out collectively. For this purpose, a certain part of the sovereignty of the individual is delegated to a select group appointed to function for all in such matters. This is the place of the State in a democracy. Such a State is perfect only to the extent to which the constituent members of the State lose their personal individual interests. They have to be self-less. Here is the call for sacrifice and dedication worthy of our Master. Will the Christian youth respond ? Civil servants in such a State will have nowhere to lay their heads. They cannot aspire to bribe-proof princely salaries but will have their bare necessities supplied by those whom they serve. How many of our Christian young people will take to the service of the masses on such terms ?

A State so constituted will provide the co-ordination needed for the satisfactory fulfilling of the economic activities of the people. Generally, the purpose of production will be to supply the wants of the masses and the State will co-ordinate individual efforts by supplying raw materials from mines and forests maintained by the State, and will provide means of communication, transportation and power, and will regulate distribution and consumption. The mineral and forest resources themselves need to be carefully husbanded by the State. The former being an exhaustible reservoir, its use has to be economically regulated, and the latter, being an everflowing current, calls for proper channelling if it is to be inexhaustible. Production will be divested of all exploitation as the units of private enterprise will be strictly limited to the capacity — financial and technical — of the masses. The centralized key industries, the exploitation of natural resources etc., will be reserved for the State. The price mechanism will be set its limits and will not be the only regulating factor of man's activities, nor will money be the sole medium of exchange. Exchange will be a well balanced system moderated by barter and payment in kind to ensure equality of bargaining power between the buyer and the seller.

Consumption will not be artificially stimulated but will be calculated to maintain the efficient functioning of man's body, mind and spirit. We do not require a collar and tie to ward us from inclement weather, nor lipstick and plucked brows to make us presentable, nor yet fork and spoon to digest our food. Such fashions are decreed to stimulate the market for unwanted goods in the interests of the producer and not in those of the consumer. Why need we hug the chains that bind us to the earth?

Every country will supply its own primary needs and turn its raw materials into consumable goods and exchange only the surplus of these with other countries for such of their production as cannot be made locally.

An economy of permanence should not have to waste the bulk of a nation's productive powers on armaments directed towards destruction and the holding down of other nations of the world for its own selfish ends. Each nation should have free play for using its talents and progressing towards the bringing of the kingdom of heaven on earth, ushering in peace and goodwill toward man.

To achieve this end, no peace treaties, agreements between nations, nor the crushing out of existence our unwanted competitors, will ever help one whit. What is needed is, not even materials for reconstruction, but a band of men who are willing to present themselves as living sacrifices, holy, acceptable to God, not conforming to this world but being transformed by renewing the mind and being born again, as Nicodemus was required to do, changing the attitude towards life and becoming universe centred by getting into tune with the Infinite. Thus shall we obtain a chosen generation, a royal priesthood and a peculiar people to leaven the earth. Unfortunately to-day, those of us who call ourselves "Christians" have accepted Western ways and, having come under the tutelege of European mentors, have learnt to ape their fashions and manner of living. Our eyes are covered with scales that make us blind to the true light which enlightens the world. Having lost our bearings, we are proceeding headlong to the precipice. We may yet repent and harken to Jesus' voice calling "Forsake all, take up thy cross and follow me". If we do, we shall have to turn our way towards the narrow and strait path and dedicate our lives to the service of the masses, expecting nothing in return; then shall we be privileged to hear the Lord say to us "inasmuch as ye have done it unto one of the least of these my brethren, ye have done it unto me".

TABULAR PRESENTATION OF CHAPTER I

ECONOMY OF TRANSIENCE

Predation	Enterprise	Gregarianism
Wild Animals of Prey (Lions, Tigers, Monkeys)	Beavers, Ants, Bees	Packs, Herds, Flock (Wolves, Elephants, Sheep)
Human: Nomadic (Hunting, fishing)	Human: Agricultural	Human: Tribal
Characteristics No contribution, Self-centred, Unitary, Emphasis on rights and indulgence	Characteristics Some contribution and use of talents Self—centred, Unitary, Emphasis on rights and accumulation of capital and indulgence	Characteristics Group interest, Team spirit, Heterogeneous, Emphasis on rights and sense of loyalty and duty towards the group and limited service and sacrifice
Principle	**Principle**	**Principle**

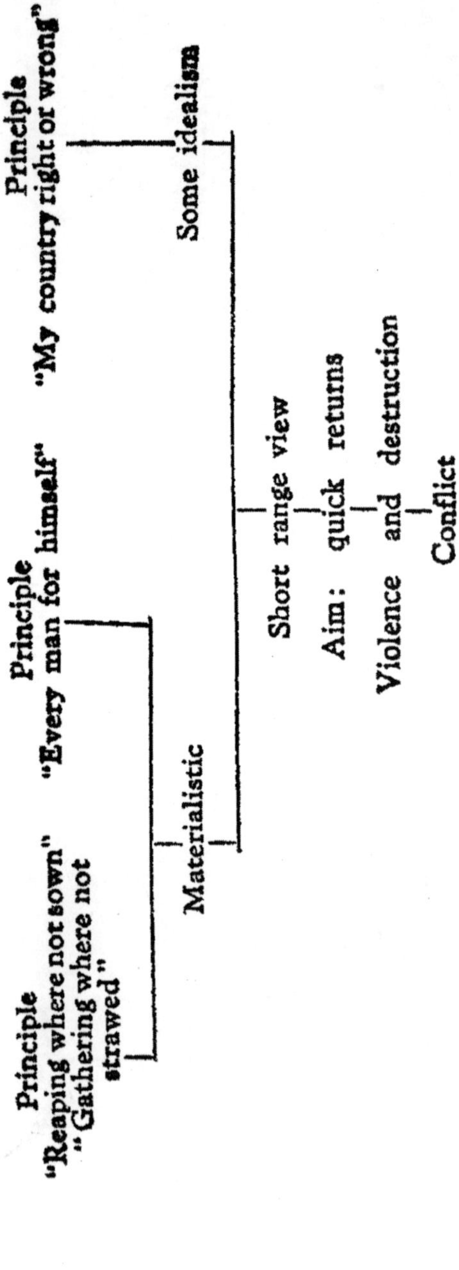
Principle
"Reaping where not sown"
"Gathering where not strawed"
Principle
"Every man for himself"
Principle
"My country right or wrong"
Materialistic
Some idealism
Short range view
Aim: quick returns
Violence and destruction
Conflict

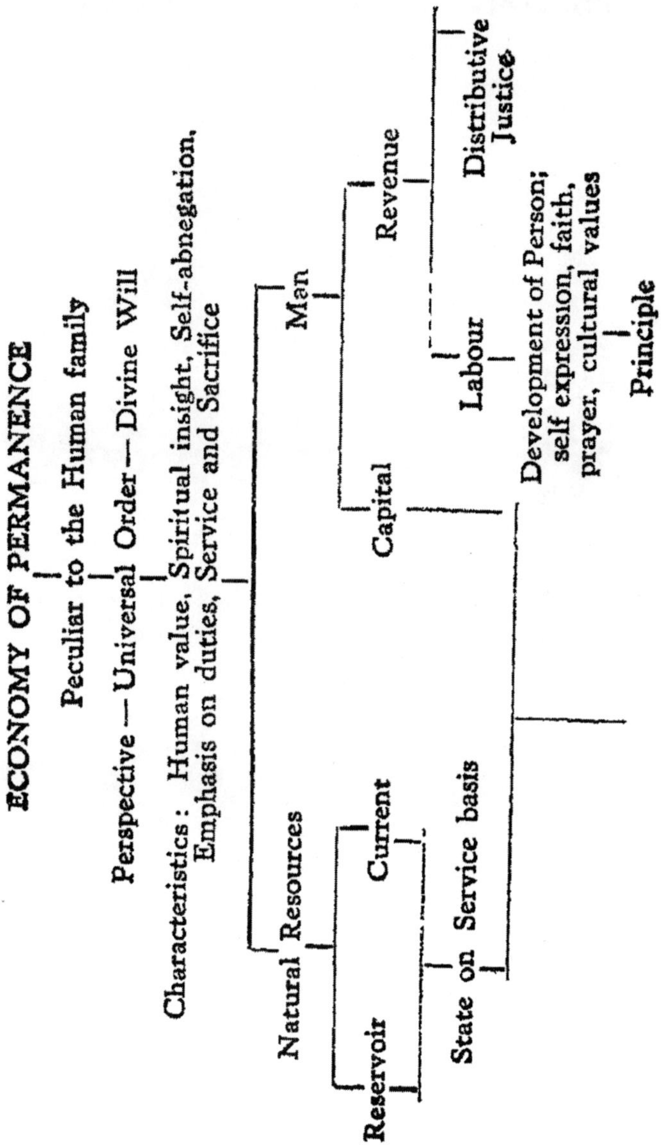
ECONOMY OF PERMANENCE
Peculiar to the Human family
Perspective — Universal Order — Divine Will
Characteristics: Human value, Spiritual insight, Self-abnegation, Emphasis on duties, Service and Sacrifice
Natural Resources
Man
Reservoir
Current
Capital
Revenue
State on Service basis
Labour
Distributive Justice
Development of Person; self expression, faith, prayer, cultural values
Principle

Principle

"Seek ye first the Kingdom of God"
"World vs. Soul"

Long range view

Aim: In tune with the In inite

Love and peace

GOODWILL, CIVILIZATION, AND PROGRESS

II

ACCEPTABLE WORKSHIP

(*Being a summary of the Inaugural Address at the Annual Camp of the Student Christian Movement at Rasulia, Hosangabad, C. P. October 1941*).

IMPLICATIONS OF THE THEME

This being the first meeting of the camp we have to spend a few moments to clarify the implications of the main theme of the Conference viz, "India's Challenge to Christian Youth."

India can be determined geographically, geologically, botanically, and in hundred and one other ways; but I take it we want to restrict ourselves to the human family, and even within that limited sphere I have to confine myself to its economic aspect or its wealth producing and distributing activities.

In the world of work it is the people that matter. Who are the people? It may be ourselves — well-fed, and cared-for town-dwellers — or the half-starved poverty-striken villagers. If we go by the largest number, we must concern ourselves with the latter because they form the major portion of India's population.

In the Report of the Industrial Survey Committee of the Government of the Central Provinces the *per capita* income of a villager is stated to be about Rs. 12 per annum. How many of you can live on Re. 1 per month? Perhaps we spend that or more per day. I have seen old women gathering grass seeds, for a gruel to keep the sides of the stomach apart. When we consider India's challenge, let us keep these starving masses in our mind. It is their challenge, that we have to consider.

'Christian' Defined: What do we mean by "Christian"? Here again there are several interpretations possible. There are the professional Christians who say "Lord, Lord" and live like lords. There are others who adhere to the Church—the Mistress of the State—with the hope of preferment and so on; but I propose to confine myself to Jesus' definition, "Whosoever shall do the will of my Father which is in heaven the same is my brother, and sister and mother". Jesus points out in a parable what the will of the Father is when the invitation to heaven is given. "Come ye blessed of my Father, inherit the kingdom prepared for you from the foundation of the world; for I was an hungred, and ye gave me meat: I was thirsty and ye gave me drink: I was a stranger and ye took me in: naked and ye clothed me: I was sick and ye visited me: I was in prison and ye came unto me." "Verily I say unto you, in as much as ye have done it unto one of the least of these my brethren ye have done it unto me." These are the duties devolving on youth who style themselves "Christians". Our land is full of the hungry, the thirsty, the down-trodden, the unclad, the sick and the oppressed. Shall we pass these by on the other side or shall we obey Jesus' command "Give ye them to eat"? Jesus says today to us as he did to Simon, son of Jonas, "Lovest thou me — Feed my lambs". Are we ready to follow him "who went about doing good and healing all that were oppressed for God was with him"? This is the full implication of the theme. Put in Jesus' words it may well read, "Sell whatsoever thou hast and give to the poor and come, take up the cross and follow me", and this is the challenge to us. Shall we also like the rich young ruler turn away sorrowful for we have great possessions?

THE DECIDING FACTORS

Our decision will be according to the plane in which we choose to live and have our being—animal, human or the spiritual—and according to the standards of value we adopt.

The Animal Plane—In crude nature, animals are not hampered by considering what effect the gratification of their needs has on others. They are purely self-centred and live in the present. Imperialism and Capitalism have given full play to this mode of life. They have built up the glories of ancient Rome and modern London and New York on a foundation of human skeletons. They have artificially stimulated and multiplied human needs, educating the masses to gratify them, caring little for anything else than their animal existence. Like Cain people have been made to feel no responsibility towards their neighbours. "Am I my brother's keeper?" is heard again and again throughout the world today. The result of this philosophy of life is seen clearly in Europe, America and Japan at present. Violence has been placed on the throne and the nations of the earth are falling down before the golden calf and worshipping it. All things are judged by money standards, and ostentatious life is the goal of the ambitious ones. Yet a few hear through all this turmoil a still small voice say, "Thou fool, this night thy soul shall be required of thee; then whose shall those things be, which thou hast provided?"

I am afraid the Indian Christian Community — and it is not alone in this respect — has been following apishly in the footsteps of their imperial masters to pick up a few crumbs that may fall from the festive board of the exploiters. It maintains a western standard of life so as to gain their respect and patronage. There is, I am glad to say, a tendency in the younger generation to break away from this, but it is still a smoking flax.

The Human Plane — With the awakening of a sense of moral value there is an attempt to include some little responsibility for the brother. The sense of duty pervades a family or a nation. There is a certain amount of ritualistic and respectable religious life, but love for the neighbour does not extend much farther than the group. The considerations are over-weighted on the family side. Such say, "Suffer me first to go and bury my father or bid them farewell which are at home." Sharp comes the reply, "Let the dead bury their dead. Follow me. No man, having put his hand to the plough, and looking back, is fit for the kingdom of God."

Many of us are in this position. Our family cares and crushing responsibilities prevent us from doing that which the highest in us bids us do. " He that loveth father or mother more than me is not worthy of me and he that loveth son or daughter more than me is not worthy of me and he that taketh not his cross and followeth after me is not worthy of me." We manage to rise above the material considerations of the animal plane, but the care of this world and the deceitfulness of riches, choke the word and we become unfruitful as we are not prepared to take up the cross daily and follow Him. Like the Gergesenes, we prefer the swine to the well-being of the neighbours and beseech Jesus that He should depart out of our coasts.

The Spiritual Plane — When the scales fall off from our eyes we realize that man does not live by bread alone. Other standards of value possess us and we ask, " What is a man profited, if he shall gain the whole world, and lose his own soul ?" The economic truth of Jesus' remark in regard to the widow who out of her penury cast in two mites into the treasury that she had cast in more than they all becomes clear to us and we realize that life is more than meat and the body more than raiment. This spiritual plane represents the attitude of Jesus — an attitude which His followers should emulate.

Their actions should be such as to uplift the lives of others and not hamper them. Jesus says, " Whoso shall offend one of these little ones, it were better for him that a millstone were hanged about his neck and that he were drowned in the depth of the sea."

Standards of Value — In this spiritual plane actions are judged, not by their material value nor by the way they satisfy human wants, but by their inner meaning, and by projecting present actions into the future and evaluating them by eternal principles. This is no new method of appraisal. You will recall how thousands of years ago King David in the cave of Adullam longed for a drink of water of the well of Bethlehem that was at the gate. At this time he was at war with the Philistines who had camped between him and Bethlehem. Three men of valour who had heard the King's wish broke through the enemy camp risking their lives and brought back to the King a pot of water from that well for the King to drink. But King David would not drink of it, but poured it out to the Lord saying " My God forbid it me that I should do this thing. Shall I drink the blood of those men that have put their lives in jeopardy to bring this ?" Valued from the animal plane a pot of water is a pot of water and nothing more. The second stage would consider it an excellent thing to be able to quench thirst by such coveted liquid, while to the spiritual eye it is no longer a simple H2. O. but is red human blood and is poured out in sacrifice in God.

Again you will remember how in Bethany in the house of Simon the leper when a woman anointed Jesus' feet with very valuable ointment from an alabaster box, Judas resented the waste of money but Jesus approved the symbolism of it. We have already mentioned Jesus' evaluation of the widow's mite.

The merchant judges a thing by its intrinsic value, a householder by sentiment and emotion but the spiritual man has to value everything according to the setting in eternity. We can attain this faculty only through prayer and fasting. In other words, it is a cultured standard of values.

We have to take up the gauntlet in this spirit and consider how we can respond to India's call.

THE TASK

To feed and clothe India's millions seems a stupendous task, and we may well ask with the disciples of Jesus "Whence should we have so much bread in the wilderness, as to fill so great a multitude?" Let us have faith and start work in our own neighbourhood. If an iota of doubt or fear enters our heart, we shall also sink like Peter on the water.

The Plan of Work—Gandhiji has unfolded a blue print for the work before us, and let each one of us find our own little corner and shed our light in our immediate surroundings so that they may see our good works and glorify the Father Which is in heaven.

This problem may be approached from the point of production and from that of consumption.

Production—As we have seen the poverty of the masses is appalling. So this immediately rules out all manner of work that calls for capital of such amounts as are beyond the financial capacity of the people. It also suggests that the emphasis should be on distribution of wealth rather than on the accumulation of wealth. These factors immediately point towards accepting decentralized methods of production.

Centralized methods of production, by their very nature, call for control of raw materials, control of a regimented labour force and control of markets. For this purpose violence has to be organized, people have to be held in bondage and exploited. Articles produced by the use of these methods, therefore, viewed from the cultural and spiritual standpoint, are soaked in human blood. Shall we like King David reject these or gorge with it with scales on our eyes?

Khadi and village-made articles distribute wealth in the process of production and demand no control over other peoples' lives.

Prices — Even intrinsically the articles produced by this method can be proved to be cheaper than articles produced by centralized methods, for the selling price of the former includes all costs while the so-called selling price of mill products only concerns itself with the out-of-pockets of the mill owner and reveals nothing of the fortunes spent by the public to make such production possible. For instance, Government spends out of taxes collected to carry on researches on the production of that variety of cotton or sugarcane most needed for mills, they provide railways, ocean routes and protect them by maintaining the army, navy and the air force. If these public costs were added, the prices would aggregate to such staggering figures that no individual could ever hope to pay for these.

To these money values may be added the cultural cost. The price of wars and innocent human blood shed in such conflicts and the cultural degradation of glorification of violence and the spreading of hatred by well-designed propaganda, who shall compute these in terms of money? What shall we give in exchange for our soul?

Consumption—Some of us may not be producers but everyone of us is a consumer. What is the duty of a consumer? Does a payment in money relieve him of all his obligations to the producer? You cannot buy your redemption by saying "It is Corban", and wash your hands of all responsibility. When we buy an article we buy with it all the conditions of production that have gone to making it. If it is produced by slave labour, we become party to such slavery; if it is manufactured by holding other people in political bondage we are partners in such imperialism;

if it is marketed by violence we are guilty of shedding human blood. How many of us are prepared to shoulder such heavy costs and pay the price ? If we are not, how can we flee from the abomination of the desolation ?

SPIRITUAL SWADESHI

If, because of our limitations, we are unable to guarantee that the articles we need are produced under coditions we would approve of, the course open to us is simple. Do not buy any article of whose conditions of production you are not aware. Limit your wants and exercise self-control. These may lead to hardship. That· is your cross. Take it and follow the Master who had not where to lay his head. The disciple is not above his Master. Simplification of life is our watchword and not gratification of all desires. "Strait is the gate and narrow is the way, which leadeth unto life." "Wide is the gate and broad is the way that leadeth to destruction."

Such restriction of consumption to articles that we can guarantee naturally limits us to goods produced in our neighbourhood. This is true swadeshi. It is not based on any hatred of foreigners and their production, but is founded on our own inability to assume responsibility for the conditions of production beyond our ken.

There is no asceticism is this simplicity. It is just a recognition of the wise man's saying:

"Better is a dinner of herbs where love is than a stalled ox and hatred therewith."
"Better is a dry morsel, and quietness therewith, than a house full of good cheer with strife."

EMPLOYMENT

Apart from taking on himself all the responsibility for the conditions of production of the goods, the consumer's act of buying also directs employment into different channels. Feeding a people does not mean buying bread and distributing it free. This may result in indiscriminate charity. We may more effectively feed a family by offering it opportunities of employment. Every one who spends an anna directs industries. If we buy toys from Japan we direct employment to that country more effectively than any Director of Industry. If we want to feed the half-starving masses of our country we must buy articles produced by them. By so doing we shall be obeying the command of Jesus, "Give ye them to eat."

Cultural Effect — Unemployment is demoralizing and work affords outlet for one's talents to develop. It gives room for initiative, resourcefulness, forethought and the 'creative faculty. It is far more effective educationally than the mere acquiring of the three R's. By providing the scope for employment we give the people the chance of self-development, self-control, self-support and self-respect.

Self-Discipline —All this cannot be undertaken without much self-discipline. The path is a hard one and calls for much forbearance. We have to lose our life to find it. "Sell whatsoever thou hast and give to the poor" means in our case "Give up all material preferments and devote your life for the poor". How many of us are willing to rise to the occasion? "The harvest truly is plenteous, but the labourers are few." Our body is indeed a temple and our faculties are entrusted to us. When we use these for our own gratification we shall be guilty of making the temple of God into a den of thieves.

True Religion — Religion does not begin and end with going to Church and making long prayers. These have their places, but we have to worship God in the need of those around us. In the words of Tagore:

Leave this chanting and singing and telling of beads,

Open thine eyes and see thy God is not before thee,

He is there where the tiller is tilling the hard ground,

And where the pathmaker is breaking stones,

He is with them in sun and in shower,

And His garment is covered with dust,

Put off thy holy mantle,

And even like Him come down on the dusty soil.

Conclusion: Wherever we turn we see skeletons walking, wherever we look we find poverty, ignorance, disease and want. Is it nothing to us? I know it is a hard saying few can bear. But this is India's call. Will it fall on deaf ears? We cannot follow any principle without crucifying our natural desires. Taking up the cross does not imply doing *puja* every day to two cross sticks. It calls for giving up all that counts for comfort and luxury, family and friends, and losing life itself to find it. If we respond to India's call we have to renounce all and serve the villagers. Help them in their production, help to market their goods, and as far as possible use only such goods as are produced by them. When time shall be no more, shall we merit "Well done, good and faithful servant, enter thou into the joy of thy Lord? For in as much as ye have done it unto the least of these, ye have done it unto me."

III

SWORDS OR PLOUGHSHARES?

(*Being the summary of a speech delivered before the Golden Jubilee Convention of the Christian Endeavour Union of India, Burma, and Ceylon, held at Indore on 8th October 1938.*)

The subject chosen for today is one of paramount importance. The world is in a turmoil. On all sides we hear of wars and rumours of wars. Nations are rising against nations, and kingdoms against kingdoms. There are famines and pestilences in diverse places. These are symptoms of the economic crisis in the world. What is the place in such a world for Jesus, the embodiment of Love and Truth, and the Prince of Peace? As possible leaders of the next generation this question challenges your attention and demands your serious and prayerful consideration. Let us, therefore, pause for a moment and analyse the various factors involved in this problem and see if there is any incompatibility between the present methods of production and the principles that Jesus stood for which will account for all this turbulence.

Since the days when Adam was told "In the sweat of thy brow shalt thou eat bread" there has been a definite effort to eat bread but to avoid sweating. Work has been looked upon as a curse and, in as much as it cannot be avoided as long as bread is needed, all manner of devices have been resorted to to pass on the unpleasant part to someone else.

ANALYSIS OF WORK

When we analyse work we do not find it a curse in itself. It has two important components (1) the germ of growth, i. e. an element which makes for the development and happiness of the individual, and (2) drudgery. Just as any seed may have the pericarp and the starch, and even as any balanced diet needs both the concentrates and the roughage to make it wholesome, work needs both its component parts to enable one to benefit by it. As the saying goes, genius is one percent inspiration and ninety nine percent perspiration. Without the perspiration or drudgery the inspiration cannot become effective. One has to have both to benefit by it. The drudgery part of work is essential to enable one to grow through work. A musician has to practise hundreds of hours on his instrument before he can venture to perform on the stage. A scientist has to labour years in a laboratory and cultivate a sense of smell which will appreciate sulphurated hydrogen; only then will he be able to probe into the secrets of nature. These are inevitable. Therefore, there can be growth only when the pleasurable part of work is combined with the drudgery. One who avoids drudgery will not gain by the pleasurable part only. Though one may enjoy it for a time, one's talents will begin to deteriorate after a while. In addition to this growth-yielding characteristic, when properly used, work functions as an outlet to the personality of the individual; it gives expression to that which is highest in man while at the same time developing his faculties. Whatever ideals, principles, or religion a man may adhere to are reflected in his everyday work. Thus there is action and reaction between the individual and his work. The reaction on the individual is perhaps much more important than the work done because it goes to develop human personality and thereby contributes to human progress.

Naturally, the drudgery part of work being unpleasant, human nature being what it is, there is always an attempt to avoid it or shift it on to someone else. The first temptation before even Jesus, was to command stones to be made bread without sweating for it. But as no one is willing to take on the drudgery part of work for what it is, it becomes necessary for those who want only the pleasurable part to use coercion, to shift the drudgery on to others. If we set out merely to enjoy life we shall have to force someone else to take up the drudgery part of work at the threat of the taskmaster's whip. Western nations have made no attempt to overcome this divorce of the pleasurable germ from the drudgery part of work. On the other hand, they have definitely set out to glorify the pleasures of life, which in itself meant enslavement of others. It was on such a philosophy of work that the ancient empires of Greece and Rome worked, shifting the unpleasant part of activity, by which pleasures can be had, on to captives made into slaves. Similarly during the Feudal days the lords got drunk and the serfs laboured. It was a sign of distinction to enjoy without working. Again under the financial regime the capitalist and the executives enjoyed, at the cost of the factory drudge. When we come to the Political age we see empires enjoying at the cost of their colonies and subject countries. The whole of this system is based on violence. Without violence no nation can shift its drudgery to other nations and convert them into "hewers of wood and drawers of water." Even Jesus was tempted to obtain the glories of the world, by what seemed a simple formula, but quickly turned away from the idea. Thus violence is the centre of the present organization or the foundation stone of the economic structure today.

But it does not stop there. The ones who enjoy the pleasures through such dissection of work are not the masses. These common people will not take to violence naturally unless their understanding is warped and their sensitiveness blunted by deliberate false propaganda. To achieve this it becomes necessary to glorify violence. This is done by giving a social status to those who are employed in applying violence on a "scientific" and mass scale, and giving such violence religious recognition. A general, an admiral or any officer in the forces is given a social standing to obtain the respect of the common people. Memorials to such men when dead are placed in places of worship to associate them with the saints and they are made national heroes by the erecting of public statues and tombs.

VIOLENCE GLORIFIED

To such an enthronement of violence what will be the reaction of Jesus who taught us that anger was equivalent to murder and to say "Thou fool" was to come in danger of hell fire ? He would regard army men as scientific murderers and generals and admirals as arch-murderers. If He went into St. Pauls Cathedral or Westminster Abbey, and saw the monuments there to these arch-murderers, He would overturn them ,like He did the money changers' tables in the Temple, saying "Ye have made the house of prayer into a den of arch-murderers ." And when we see the tattered banners of many a battle decorating those sacred walls, do we not hear the reverberations of the echo of the two thousand year old cry, "Away with this man, release unto us Barabbas." Now Barabbas was a murderer and a robber. A social structure which sanctifies violence has crucified Jesus already. It is such "cultures" we find in Europe, in battle array, growling at each other at the present moment. What does this appeal to might mean ? Is this to make the world safe for democracy ? Or is it a war to end war ? We cannot cast out devils through the Prince of devils. All they that take the sword shall perish with the sword. What is all this degradation of the soul of man for ?

IN PRACTICE

All this is to shift the drudgery and unpleasant part of work on to some one else. To do so we have to produce under controlled conditions on a large scale. Though the Lancashire mill is located in England, its ramifications extend the world over. To work it therefore we need world-wide control of the cotton growing soils, farmers, the research institutes, the railway rates, ports, steamships, ocean routes and bases like Singapore, Aden and Gibralter and markets too have to be controlled. Without such world wide domination the Lancashire mill cannot be worked for one day. Such complete and wide-spread political control necessitates the Army, Navy and the Air force. Hence it is that without violence England cannot maintain itself on the present level any more than a tiger can feed itself without its claws or fangs. This is the position with all countries based on centralized methods of production. They have to deprive other people of freedom so that the latter may be converted into slaves to produce the raw materials they need and consume the goods they manufacture. Thus it is that we find the nations of Europe and Japan parting the garments and casting lots on India, China, Abysinnia and Czechoslovakia today. This economic condition is the cause of the violence with which the atmosphere is now surcharged and has been for over a generation. Science has been harnessed to the forces of destruction and "except these days be shortened there should no flesh be saved." The philosophy behind our present economic structure is "what matters if the soul is lost as long as the whole world is gained." The vested interests of today care more for their swine than for the life of the man out of whom the devils were cast out. They beseech Jesus to depart from their coasts. As long as Jesus is out of the equation there can be nothing but conflict. There has never been peace in Europe. It is always a case of dynamic war or static war as there is no basis for peace in suspicion and hatred. Peace can only come from love and goodwill.

THE ALTERNATIVE

While the centralized method of production need violence as an essential factor, production by decentralized units can be carried on without resorting to violence. Of course by this method we cannot produce highly standardized goods hence the quantity produced will be less than what can be obtained under centralized units, but at the same time the quality and the individuality or variety can be much greater under the cottage unit. This latter method also makes it possible for the two elements of work *viz.* development and drudgery, to be functioning in a normal way thus making for human progress. Because of the capacity of the present method to produce standardized goods in large quantities, the producers have been carrying on a propaganda to increase their sales by making people buy their goods. To do this a tradition has been introduced making the multiplicity of wants a sign of civilization and culture. Is possession of great wealth the equivalent of happiness and welfare either in this world or in the world to come? Do not the cares of this world and the deceitfulness of riches choke that which is noblest in us? What then is the remedy?

The remedy lies in our getting away from the idea that a man's life consisteth in the abundance of the things which he possesseth and being ready if our right hand offends us to cut it off and cast it from us. May we have the courage to face this situation and not turn away sorrowful because of our great possessions? Is not life more than meat? Is there not a human value which is higher than any material standards? If we decide to follow this higher value we shall have to take up the cross of many material inconveniences and follow Jesus in His path of truth, love and peace. If we follow Jesus' ideals we shall neither hunger nor thirst after material possessions.

TRUE VALUES

Jesus evaluated things according to the use they were to individual human beings. To him the widow's two mites were more than all the rest, for, she of her penury had cast in all the living that she had. If we love our neighbours as ourselves we shall be able to realize and appreciate the true value of all that we possess. If we long for articles that are made by depriving nations of their freedom, by resorting to violence, by devouring widows' houses, by taking the taxes from the poor to serve the needs of the rich, we shall be ignoring Jesus' standards, and gaining materially at the cost of the suffering of others. As Solomon says:

"Better is little with the fear of the Lord
than great treasure and trouble therewith,"
"Better is little with righteousness
than great revenues without right".

Shall we save our life or lose it? If we are convinced that the present atmosphere of war is caused by the desire to control raw materials and markets we shall be parties to violence and bloodshed if we subscribe to it by buying or selling goods made under such methods. So if we wish to usher in peace and goodwill among nations we shall have to remember that the Master we profess to follow had not where to lay his head. The servant cannot be greater than the master. What shall be our choice? The broad path or the narrow way? Hitler or Gandhiji? Barabbas or Jesus? The sword or the ploughshare?

IV

PROSELYTISING

(*Being the report of a speech delivered before the Council of the Federation of International Fellowships, at its session at Wardha on 29th Dec.* 1935.)

The problems of conversion cannot be dealt with either as a "spiritual change" or as a "change of community" without the principle itself being considered and understood, as otherwise we shall be merely begging the question. The meaning of the term conversion itself has deen used in many senses. Similarly, also the words "Religion" and "God". According to our individual conceptions of God and the functions of a religion, the purpose of conversion also will differ. I am afraid, it will be beyond me to attempt a metaphysical discussion. I can only put forward my own personal understanding of the situation in the light of the teachings of Jesus, as recorded by various Gospel writers. We have to bear in mind that even here we are dependent on the frail media of the unsophisticated disciples of Jesus. In the preceding discussions we have been using the word religion in two senses, with reference to both Christianity and Hinduism. In the ancient world, religion played the part of a code of laws, regulating people's daily conduct and mode of life. In this sense, Judaism and Hinduism are religions, while Christianity cannot be brought into such a category. You will remember with what meticulous care the ceremonials are described in the pentateuch and in the Hindu scriptures. In this sense, Christianity is not a religion. So while a person may be a good Hindu he may yet owe allegiance to Jesus. Therefore as long as there is nothing repugnant in one religion to the tenets of another there is no cause for conversion.

In the Christian conception of God we have to remember that many attributes are merely carried over from the early days of Judaism. The tribal God of the Jews, who visited the inequity of the fathers upon the children unto the third and fourth generation, and showed mercy unto thousands of them that loved Him, still persists amongst the Christians so-called. God exists to revenge and to reward. This God has to be propitiated by extending his domain by getting adherents. Herein is the reason for conversion. For every addition to the flock we get a gem in our Crown in Heaven. This God in his turn looks after the welfare of His people on earth and fights their battles. The Western nations have four forms of arms – defensive and offensive — the army, the navy, the air force and the Church. So conversion is recruiting in the services of God, King, and country. Missionaries, I know will stoutly deny this as their main function, but they are nevertheless conscious or unconscious recruiting agents for gun-fodder. At times of conflict every pulpit is converted into a recruiting platform and the churches on either sides vie with each other to gain all they can in the Imperialistic struggle. I am reminded at this moment of the valuable services rendered by the Bishop of London who went about the front during the world war preaching that the boys who died fighting would go straight to heaven. In his speech Seth Jamnalalji pointed out that the missionaries emphasize the fact that Hinduism holds about 60 million Harijans as slaves as an excuse for their mission of conversion, while they ignore the injustice of subjecting 350 millions to bondage. In reply the British Missionary friend who spoke before me stated that they themselves are subject to the same Government. Yes, it is true; we are slaves in that our political and economic liberty is curbed under fortuitous circumstances, but the missionaries are greater slaves than we in that they have willingly sold their conscience to the Government. They fear them which kill the body but not Him which is able to destroy both soul and body in hell. Their shackles are heavier than ours. Let us pity them. How can we expect these slaves to help us to attain freedom and justice. Nobody can lift himself with his own bootstrings. During the Satyagraha Movement when all kinds of atrocities were inflicted on the Satyagrahis the Missionaries stood at a safe distance or within the precincts of the churches, and prayed to their God for peace. This is a cowardly and futile attitude. This is not the stuff of which even the church was built up in the early days. When there is no trouble they issue forth from their hiding places and preach, and attempt to convert people to cowardice. The history of the Church teaches us that she has been the handmaiden of the State through the ages. Therefore any increase in the number of her adherents strengthens the State. In this way the missionaries are playing a dangerous political game in conversion, unconsciously though it may be.

These are all perversions of Jesus 'teachings, giving rise to monstrosities in the religious sphere. Let us for a moment turn to the idea of Jesus on the subject. According to the records, we do not find that Jesus advocated any particular form of religion. He himself was not a Christian and we do not see anywhere that he advocated a change of religion as the result of spiritual transformation. True, he said a man must be born again, but this does not necessitate a change of religion. He did not recognize a tribal God, nor is it sure if he even recognized any set form of religion. He has given us a certain unit of measure. The yardstick of allegiance is, "He that is not against us is for us", and not the fact of belonging to any particular religion. "Ye shall know them by their fruits" is his criterion of conduct, and not the ceremonial adherence to baptism, etc. His mission was "Heal the sick, cleanse the lepers, raise the dead and cast out devils." All forms of social service is all that a follower can render. The test of those who belonged to his family or community is who-so-ever shall do the will of my Father which is in heaven, the same is my brother, sister and mother" irrespective of what community or religion a person may belong to. The form of worship he advocated was not the number of times one had to participate in certain rituals, but to "Let your light so shine before men that they may see your good works and glorify your Father in heaven." Where then is there room for conversion as practised by missionaries? When Saul was converted into Paul he did not change his religion. He changed from a fanatic persecutor into one "who was not against us," one who yielded good fruits, who went about serving the needy, and he rejoiced in doing the will of the Father, and lighted those in darkness.

So much for his teachings, and now let us see what Jesus said directly in regard to conversion. "Woe unto you Scribes, and Pharisees, hypocrites, for ye compass sea and land to make one proselyte and when he is made, you make him twofold more the child of hell than yourselves."

We see Jesus' idea of love of God when he says, "Simon lovest thou me, feed my lambs." God is not in need of those who honour him with the lips, saying, "Lord Lord" but only those who do the will of the Father in Heaven will be invited to inherit the Kingdom.

" For I was thirsty, ye gave me drink; I was a stranger and you took me in; naked and ye clothed me; I was in prison and ye came unto me." So the only conversion that can take place is not in the religion we adhere to, but in our attitudes to our fellowmen. On the day of reckoning, God will not ask of us our rank allegiance or birth, but just what we had done on earth. In as much as ye had done it unto the least of these my brethren ye had done it unto me." "There is neither Greek nor Jew, circumcision or uncircumcision, Barbarian Scythian, Bond or Free" neither Hindu, nor Muslim, neither Zoroastrian, nor Christians. It is our ideals that matter. If we went to convert a person it can be only to a field of service and not to any man-made fold. Each man is individually responsible to his Maker. Conversion as practised by the missionaries has no support from Jesus, as far as I can see, and it is only a mode of increasing the adherents of an institutional religion called Christianity, of which Jesus was neither the founder nor a member.

V

RELIGION OF JESUS

(*Being an Address delivered before the Parliament of Religions, Bombay in May* 1936.)

Before we consider our special topic for this evening you will bear with me if I state clearly what aspect of religion I propose to discuss. The word religion is often used to connote many social systems and organizations working towards different set goals.

AUTHORITARIAN RELIGION

In the early stages of evolution of Society, crude superstitions were bound together with inhibitions and prohibitions to regulate the primitive man and his dealings; his failings were thought to be visited with punishment from on high and his obedience with reward. Fear deterred him in his selfish ventures and avarice and desire for pleasure made him consider the welfare of others.

MILITANT RELIGION

Later on we find national codes of laws bound between social sanctions with a religious colouring. In the case of martial people we find " God exercising a tribal patronage and authority". Here too man was kept to the " right path " by an external power invested with a jealous spirit to guard its rights, and with vengeance to visit the iniquity of the fathers to the third and fourth generations of them that hate it and doing good to thousands of them that fear it. In this stage there is a definite desire on the part of the people to try to increase the numbers owning allegiance to it. Such efforts are expected to be rewarded.

ETHNICAL RELIGION

In addition to these, man uses religion in an organized form to preserve, propagate and consolidate a culture evolved by him.

SOCIAL RELIGION

With the advance of civilization religion has become a respectable code of behaviour, with recognized customs and manners. People are expected to follow certain rituals and thus retain respectability in society.

These four forms may be grouped as organized or institutional religions. Most ancient religions have gone through some or all these stages, and bear the marks to some extent of each of them. None of these interest us at the present time. The Christianity of the Western people partakes of the nature of many of these forms.

As the authoritarian religion, God in Christianity is depicted as a strict Accountant, keeping a record of all we do in a book of fate and visiting our lapses with uncompromising justice. Fear of God is said to be the beginning of wisdom. If you behave you go to Heaven, if not, you go to Hell.

Since the day Peter sought comfort and warmth by fraternizing with the servants of the great ones of earth, and was thus led into denying the Lord, the militant churches of various denominations have followed the example of their foundation-stone and have been sycophants in the courts, courtyards and lobbies of the rulers. We find them still there today. They are seeking their own warmth and comfort and are led into a continual denial of the Lord, not merely before the cock crows, but all the time. The churches are being used by the States as a convenient form of holding the people down. We find in the course of history that this leads to bitterness. We see Russia estranged from all spiritual values because of the part the Church had played in keeping the people enslaved.

Such churches are necessary adjuncts to Imperialism. We need not stray as far as Russia. Christian missions in our land, and all other " heathen " lands fall into this group naturally. It is painful to see adherents of Christianity rushing to interview disgruntled members of other religions to recruit them into their fold. They sing a song of civilizing the savage, and end up by sapping his blood, by exploiting his labour, and annexing his territory.

During the dark ages in Europe we saw Christianity functioning as an ethnical religion marshalling its forces on a crusade against the Sarscenic hordes and pagan world. The desire to bring light and learning to those who sit in darkness arises out of the ethnical form of religion, with an admixture of the imperialistic militant spirit.

Today we need no evidence of Christianity functioning as a social religion. If you want to get into the upper circle of society, membership in a Church of England chapel goes a long way. It is a sign of respectability. Even a Jew as a Viceroy had to be respectable by attending the Church of England services on State functions.

We are not going to consider Christianity in this light. Our purpose is not sociological or political. Although I do not deny that these forms of religion have served and are serving a very useful purpose in a world peopled by individuals in different stages of evolution, yet I find no evidence of Jesus having founded a religion which will fall under any of the above groups. If modern Christianity finds a place amongst them, it is a sign that Jesus had nothing to do with it in the form in which we find it today. Jesus says "My doctrine is not mine but His that sent me." If those principles are from the one God then the religion of Jesus is as universal as that God himself.

My object in touching on these primary functions of religion is to show how far Christianity has fulfilled these. In addition to these there are also a few denominations like the Society of Friends, and particular individuals who practise the principles of Jesus in an unorganized way. As we shall proceed to examine presently these principles, we shall notice that such pure interpretations of the life of Jesus are merely the exception in the religion as developed in the West.

PURE RELIGION

In the true sense religion is the relation that governs a man's personal attitude to God, to his ideals, to his fellow-man, to society and to the world. What we want to consider today is Jesus' religion in this sense. That is to say, the personal relationship of Jesus to these. When He walked on this earth, (1) what was His religion? (2) what was His attitude to God? (3) what was His conception of Himself? (4) what was His relationship to His parents and elders? (5) to His contemporaries, His brothers and sisters? (6) to Society and to the State? (7) to material possessions? (8) to human values? and (9) to other religions?

In this form of a personal spiritual union with God and the world, the religion of Jesus forms the culmination of the evolution we find in Judaism. This is pure religion, with no sociology or politics mixed with it. Some years ago Dr. J. C. Farquhar published a book "The Crown of Hinduism," where he sought to establish Christianity as the ultimate attainment of Hinduism. He tried to separate the pure religion of Jesus from its parent sociological root Judaism and to graft it on to the sociological part of Hinduism, forgetting that all pure religions are personal. For the sake of convenience we may group common experiences under a common category, but individual religion knows no label. The personal religion of our Chairman, Sir S. Radhakrishnan, that of Pandit Madan Mohan Malaviya, and that of Gandhiji, may be grouped as Hinduism for convenience, but in reality they are three different religions, with the impress or the personality of each with God. As a pebble thrown upon the bosom of the ocean causes ripples on the mighty expanse of water, a man, however small he may be, causes his impressions to be set on the Infinite.

As long as we grant that an individual has a personality of his own, his intimate relations with everyone else will be stamped with his individuality. It is futile to expect millions to follow one type of relationship with everybody. Can the friendship between any two humans be the same as the friendship of any other two? Each relationship stands on its own. They may all be called friendships for convenience, but each friendship between two personalities entering into a particular friendship provides the attributes that make that friendship. If you remove any one of them the relationship ceases to be the same, There can be no converts to religion in this sense. If Dr. Radhakrishnan and I are friends we cannot convert any others into that friendship. Similar friendship may exist, but identical ones cannot. It -is from this point of view that we wish to study the religion of Jesus.

1. JESUS' RELIGION

In the accepted meaning of the term the religion of Jesus was no religion at all as no two persons' religion can be identical. No man-made rule can bind him down against his convictions. Man was not made for Sabbath. He condemned institutional religion when it was made a means of exploitation; and in no uncertain terms he denounced the stalwarts of institutional religion. Yet, in another way, we may say that the religion of Jesus was universal, in as much as all religions have God as common factor and each person as a variant. Hear it is that all religions meet, and Sri Ramakrishna might well say, "All religions are one." To the frog in the well, its well is the only chosen well in which the sun, moon and stars are reflected, its atmosphere encircled by the walls of religious ritual is peculiarly its own, and is different from the other wells, and a zealous frog will try to recruit more companions. But to an eagle soaring the sky, all atmosphere is one, and there is room in it for all and sundry, and it realizes there is only one sky with the same sun, moon and stars for everybody.

2. JESUS' RELATION TO GOD

In regard to Jesus' relation to God, we find scattered throughout the Gospels, evidence of the religion of Jesus being a very personal religion. "When thou prayest enter into thy closet and when thou hast shut thy door, pray to thy Father which is in secret." We see that Jesus had no ideas of exclusive worship. "Ye shall neither in this mountain nor yet at Jerusalem, worship the Father. . . the true worshipper shall worship the Father in Spirit and in truth . . . . . God is a Spirit, and they that worship Him must worship Him in Spirit and in Truth.

Those who set high values on ritual to be followed by everybody deny the religion of Jesus. Spirit knows no ritual. Religion is a personal contact with God. What form it should take remains with the devotee. What suits one person will not help another. It is futile to lay down set forms and ceremonies. At the same time we have to recognize that the experiences of others are helpful to us, and there are several spirits quite close enough in their make up to be able to fall into convenient groups. Such groups may get together for common worship, for mutual aid and help, but such common forms are definitely sinful when they assume an exclusive aspect. No church or religion has any religious sanction from Jesus to say, "Unless you do as I do, you will not be saved." "He that is not against us is for us" is the broad principle laid down by Jesus.

3. BROTHERHOOD OF MAN

God is a Father, and all men are brethren. This was Jesus' ruling relationship to his fellow men. He did not regard any as an outsider. His was a universal religion. Every child born of woman, immediately attained fraternal relationship with Jesus by the very fact of its belonging to the human family. He had not to wait till the child was baptized to receive it into any group. Will any church dare deny entry to one whom Jesus claims as His brother? Where then is the foundation for conversion or closing the doors of any church against non-Christians? The so called Christian churches that claim exclusive rights have drifted far from the religion of Jesus.

"All that the Father giveth me, shall come to me, and him that cometh to me I shall in no wise cast out." In the Christian churches even today we find distinctions of colour and race made among its own members. Even after death the body of one who was a member in his lifetime of a church but who had a dark skin, cannot be buried along side the body of another member of the same church but who had a white skin. Is it not blasphemy to call such churches Christian? Such may be "White Clubs" but not churches of God.

If we wish to trace the origin of the missionary spirit in what is called Christianity we shall find it goes to St. Paul, the child of Imperial Rome, and not to Jesus the Nazarene. When Jesus sent out His disciples His charge to them was "Go not into the way of the Gentiles and into any city of the Samaritans enter ye not, but go rather to the lost sheep of the house of Israel." If we paraphrase it today it would read, "Go not to the distant parts of the world to those professing other religion, but go ra her to your own neighbours and teach them the right path." Our missionaries conveniently turn literalists when it suits them and leave out passages for generous interpretation hen it goes against them.

If literal interpretations there must be, I submit the injunctions to the disciples should be followed by preference. "Provide neither gold, nor silver, nor brass in your purse, neither scrip for your journey, neither two coats, neither shoes nor yet staves, for the workman is worthy of his meat." I would commend the missions accepting this as a test to see how near to the religion of Jesus they approximate.

How shall we know whether our relationship with God is of the right sort if each individual lays down his own standard and attitude ? "By their fruits ye shall know them" not by their professions nor their formal following of ceremonies. "Let your light so shine before men that seeing your good works they may glorify your Father in Heaven."

4. WHAT WAS JESUS' ATTITUDE TO HIMSELF ?

He considered himself a tool in the hands of God. "My meat is to do the will of Him that sent me and to finish His work" and again He says "I must work the work of Him that sent me." We find what He conceives to be the will of the Father in the instructions He gives to His disciples while sending them out. "Heal the sick, cleanse the lepers, raise the dead, cast out devils". That is Jesus' idea of our mission in life-service of our fellow men in need. This was not merely a precept. His short life was one of intense active service. He wished to be known, not as the son of David, but by the service He was rendering. When John the Baptist sent enquiring who Jesus was, the answer was "Go your way and tell John what things ye have seen and heard, how that the blind see, the lame walk, the lepers are cleansed, the dead are raised, to the poor the gospel is preached." Here is a testimony of a man's religion. When we are asked what religion we follow can we Christians say, "Look at my Western clothes, look at my cropped head, look at my Western manners; my table is laden with beef and pork, and my house is decorated with things gathered from the four corners of the earth. I go to church on Sundays and have a pew in front; our names are drawn from the saints in the Bible; I wear a cross round my neck, or on the watch chain, and read the Bible morning evening and night, and pray to God that the hungry may be fed. Will not Jesus say, "I know ye not; not everyone that saith unto me, Lord Lord, shall enter into the Kingdom of Heaven, but He that doeth the will of my Father which is in heaven." In regard to his mission he says, "To this end was I born and for this cause came I into the world, that I should bear witness unto the truth."

5. WHAT USE HAD JESUS FOR HIS ELDERS?

If we look upon religion as a close form of "Friendship" between God and man, the senior most place is given to God, to whom man owes unconditional obedience, and every other relationship has to be subordinated to this. This subordinating does not lead to any conflict, but is a natural outcome of it. If one is in close friendship with a personality like Gandhiji, that friendship is of no value unless it is reflected in all one's other relations. This cannot be helped. In the same way if we are in close communion with God, all our activities will bear the hall-mark, and our faces will be transfigured. If God claims the first place, all others come afterwards. The child Jesus can say with no disrespect to his parents "wist ye not that I must be about my Father's business" and the young man, Jesus, can say to his mother "woman, what have I to do with thee." Jesus, never followed custom just because of its age old authority. We frequently hear "It was said by them of old time .... but I say unto you". If the God relationship is a living one no other authority can supersede that; no human being, father, or mother, old or young can stand between us and the realization of our ideals. "He that loveth father or mother more than me, is not worthy of me."

There is a converse to this. Those who are in a senior position should know that it is not their due to obtain servile obedience from their juniors. The personality of each individual is sacred and has to have its own development. There can be no human authority which can claim unquestioning obedience. Churches that profess to be the conscience-keepers of their devotees will find no support in Jesus, who seeks to establish direct individual touch with the Divine.

6. WHAT OF OUR EQUALS AND OUR NEIGHBOURS?

We have to find God in the service of our brethren. We cannot play the role of interceders and raise holy hands in prayer, and ask God to relieve the suffering of others. "Simon, lovest thou me .... feed my sheep". We have to render neighbourly service. "For I was an hungered and ye gave me meat, I was thirsty and ye gave me drink: I was a stranger and ye took me in, naked and ye clothed me: I was sick and ye visited me; I was in prison and ye came unto me." This does not stop with mere supply of needs. We have to be careful of our actions that we do not lead others into the wrong by them. "It were better for him that a millstone were hanged about his neck and he be cast into the sea, than that he should offend one of these little ones."

I am afraid, Christian Churches have not been mindful of these instructions in their great hurry to make the world worship as they do. They have disregarded all other religions even where they have not actively persecuted them. Jesus would have them consider all legitimate prejudices of our neighbours. Some of the rituals now practised by the churches are revolting to the fine sentiments of the people amongst whom we live. Is it so essential to the propagating of the religion of Jesus, that amongst a vegetarian people who refrain from eating even roots that grow below the surface of the land, as such roots have more life, to practise a ritual in which the blood of the founder is symbolically drunk and his flesh is ceremonially eaten, nay, in some, they claim to consume the actual blood and flesh? These gruesome practices would have no weight in the religion of Jesus.

Jesus the compassionate, who says to the woman taken in her sin, "Neither do I condemn thee, go and sin no more" will not condemn those who are earnestly seeking to walk with God. The religion of Jesus is not a measuring rod for the "Pagan," but a helpful ladder at the disposal of everyone who wishes to use it. Wherever there was hope Jesus would encourage the struggle regardless of man made labels. "A bruised reed shall he not break, and a smoking flax shall he not quench".

7. DID JESUS HAVE ANY USE FOR STATE AND SOCIETY

From the time the church entered into an unholy alliance with the State and became its handmaiden, it has enjoined unquestioning loyalty to it. As far as we can see this was not Jesus' attitude and is not in keeping with the highly personal religion he practised. As we have seen, Jesus gave the first place to his ideal. If the State or Society went against it, then the ideals had to prevail nevertheless. The blood of martyrs through the ages will bear witness to this. He repeatedly taught those around him that man's needs were above all institutions. He openly challenged the Pharisees in regard to adherance to customs and tradition irrespective of the claims of those around. In so far as the state was working for the welfare of the people, and the people co-operated with it, it is the duty of the citizen to do his share. The State has to perform certain functions and the citizen has to find the means for it. "Render unto Caeser the things that are Caeser's and unto God the things that are God's." When the power of State or society became tyrannical, Jesus revolted against it. When Herod misused his power and position Jesus called him. "That fox" and condemned the "devouring of widows' " houses in the name of religion. He has always given the first place to the needs of the people, and in so far as the State served them, he extended his co-operation as when He asked Simon to pay the tribute money "for me and thee".

Men have tried again and again to formulate definite forms of Government from Jesus' words, but have made gross blunders, as Jesus only laid down principles and expected everyone to decide his course of action for himself, led by the spirit of Truth. Jesus left no comprehensive plan and did not claim to be the final revelation. He said, "I have yet many things to say unto you but ye cannot bear them now. Howbeit when He the spirit of Truth is come, He will guide you into all truth: . . . . and He will shew you things to come." We cannot excuse ourselves from taking part in politics. As we have already seen if our relationship with God is vital, it will make itself felt in all our relations. As long as we are members of a gregarious society we must be related politically to those among whom we have our being. To say that any religious man can promise to keep out of politics is to make a play thing of religion. Can a trained becteriologist say he will promise to have nothing to do with the sanitation and hygiene of the village in which he lives? what use then will be his knowledge? If you are in close communion with a just God will it not be impossible for you to shut your eyes to injustice to your fellowmen? Conscience cannot be locked up in steel cases at our convenience.

A missionary friend told me that if any of them protested against any political wrongs they would be sent back by the next boat.

and asked me what would become of their work. Is the God we serve impotent without us? "God is able of these stones to raise up children unto Abraham." If His work is worth doing He will see to it. All that we are asked to do is to do the will of the Father in Heaven; the consequences need not deter us.

Although Jesus Himself did not formulate any political theories etc., it is simple to apply his religion to modern requirements of Statecraft.

He lent cooperation to authority in so far as it lay along his principles and he did not hesitate to cut across all regulations when they were inimical to human interests. "The sabbath was made for man" will be the motto of civil disobedience. Where the situation called for it the religion of Jesus enjoins direct action against man-made codes of law. "Laying aside the commandments of God, ye hold the tradition of men . . . . making the word of God of none effect through your tradition." After warning His disciples of the leaven of the Pharisees he says, "Be not afraid of them that kill the body, and after that have no more that they can do".

8. MATERIAL POSSESSIONS

When the means becomes the end, there is a danger of the goal never being reached. Jesus valued material possessions only as a means of achieving His ideals. He found the money to pay tribute, "lest we should offend them". The moment we set our hearts on the means, property becomes an evil. It is easier for a camel to go through the eye of a needle than for a rich man to enter into the kingdom of heaven. When property makes us lose all sense of proportion it becomes a danger. For one who has to work for the kingdom, property is a hindrance and one has to relieve oneself of it just as a swimmer casts off all unnecessary garments. The casting off of the garment itself is no virtue, but lightens the burden on the way. We earn no merit by ascetism itself. He reminded those who sought him for worldly benefits that "foxes have holes and the birds of the air have nests, but the son of man hath not where to lay his head." This ought to be the answer to any who wish to embrace Christianity for worldly considerations. The one danger of material possessions is the feeling of satisfaction one seeks in it, and the way its acquisition absorbs all thought and action, "Where your treasure is, there will your heart be also". what shall it profit a man if he gain the whole world and lose his own soul? We are so built that it is not possible to divide our attention equally between worldly matters and spiritual claims. We cannot serve God and mammon.

9. HUMAN VALUES

When we talk of religion we often lose sight of our physical side. The religion of Jesus is quite alive to the needs of the man. In dealing with the soul the body is not forgotten. Jesus does not deal with man in bulk but applies his general principles in relation to each individual. The principles of themselves possess no virtues but assume importance only in relation to particular human beings. We see Jesus watching the gifts cast into the temple treasury. He values the two mites of the poor widow more than all the others. He goes by the relative values or as an economist will put it by the marginal utility. Our gifts and services are valued by the purity of their motives. In the parable of the talents the same principle of valuation is shown. Every man is judged and dealt with according to his own ability. While this may be a consolation to some, to others it is a grave situation. for "unto whomsoever much is given of him much shall be required." This principle cuts at the root of uniform religious observances and emphasizes the personal aspect of religion. The religion of Jesus is not an impersonal set form of conduct, but adjusts itself to the ability of the individual to see God. Therefore none of us can have any grounds to condemn anyone. It is also impossible for us to judge who will go to heaven and who to hell merely by the conduct of the individual. There are no absolute standards to go by. Rules and regulations which are intended for the conduct of the people, are subordinate to the needs of the individual. In the observing of the letter of the law we ought not to cause offences to any of our brethren. The main thing is the fulfilment of the spirit in relation to the needs of the people. The right of way is to human needs. Life is more than meat, and the body more than raiment.

10. OTHER RELIGIONS

In the religion of Jesus there is no intolerance of other forms of religion. He was very impatient of over-zealous Jews, because of their narrow religious outlook. He himself sent his disciples to the lost sheep of the house of Israel and not to the Gentiles. He denounced the Scribes and Pharisees, "for ye compass sea and land to make one proselyte and when he is made ye make him two-fold more the child of hell than yourselves."

The religion of Jesus was not exclusive, "I say unto you, that men will come from the east and from the west, and shall sit down with Abraham and Issac and Jacob in the kingdom of heaven, but the children of the kingdom shall be cast out."

In the parable of the Good Samaritan, Jesus gives the place of honour and esteem to one who is not a Jew but the Harijan of the day. It indicates Jesus' desire to bring forward such despised people.

What weighs with Jesus is not the allegiance of any individual to any particular religion but the individual's attitude to his fellow men.

In the earlier part of the address I had referred to Dr. Farquhar's "Crown of Hinduism." Now that we have analysed the Religion of Jesus we can understand why Dr. Farquhar was looking for a head to place the crown. Although we said that Christianity may be looked upon as the Crown of Judaism, yet we cannot accept the personal religion of Jesus such as the one we have formulated here, as the crown of Christianity. Christianity has developed into a smug, comfortable, selfish and individualistic religion, seeking for its own gain. While the religion of Jesus requires for its growth the background of a collective social order, such as we find Hinduism has developed in India. To cite one instance, take even the joint family system, where the fit and the unfit, the rich and the poor, the gifted and the incapable, all live together and share a common purse. This system has its weakness, but it is distinctly an attempt towards loving thy neighbour as thyself. Again amongst the usulmans there is neither black, white or brown, prince, peasant or pauper. All practice a democracy which puts to shame the race for the High places in Christianity. We can see Dr. Farquhar was conscious that there was a need for a head fitted to receive the Religion of Jesus, and found it not in Christianity, but in the social order evolved by Hinduism. Of course the pure personal religion of Jesus needs a sociological order suited to it to take root. As we have noticed except in cases such as that of the Society of Friends it does not find a congenial, well prepared ground to germinate in western forms of modern Christianity.

We have looked at the religion of Jesus from various aspects. When we study the pure form, we notice in every feature of it a similarity to the culture of India. On the other hand, Christianity, as we see around us, is totally foreign to our culture. The gorgeous ceremonies, the dependence on the priesthood, the aggressive proselytizing spirit and the obeisance the church pays to state are not found in our land. Amongst us, individual or family worship, with simple forms and rites, performed by the devotee himself, without the intervention of a priest, commonly in the home itself, is the general form of worship. Westerners have centralized even their religion. In every walk of life our ways are decentralized; so was that of Jesus. The religion of Jesus was highly individualistic, while the Christian churches are masterpieces of centralized organization and administration. Many of the prelates spend their time not in prayer and meditation but in the cares of administration. They have turned Marthas; Marys will flourish only in the religion of Jesus. Even for the worker the way prescribed by Jesus is much the same as is practised today in india. "Into whatsoever city or town ye shall enter, enquire who in it is worthy, and there abide till ye go thence." To this day our social workers depend on such hospitality. Can the churches afford to follow Jesus literally here? In India it is nothing strange. Poverty, prescribed by Jesus, is honoured in our land. The churches cannot carry on their work on that basis. All these variations prove how far from the religion of Jesus the churches have drifted. In the Indian culture the fields are ready unto harvest for the pure religion of Jesus, but there is no room for modern Christianity.

In conclusion we may say that the religion of Jesus teaches that:—Neither in the cathedral, church or chapel, nor in the mosque, tabernacle or temple, do we need to worship God. The true worshiper shall worship God in spirit and truth, the label and the special brand do not matter.

2. We are not to seek out converts in distant lands but help the wayward ones around us to lead a better life by our own living example.

3. God judges us not by our professions or by our allegiance but by our actions and services to those in need.

4. We have to work out our ideals irrespective of the obstacles in the way.

5. True worship is service of suffering humanity without counting the cost.

6. Each person will be judged on his own merits. There is no universal standard.

7. The whole human family is one under the selfsame Father.

Thus we find that Jesus practised and preached a personal religion which derived its characteristics from his attitude to God, and his conception of his mission. The greatest had to be the servant of all. No human need was to be sacrificed to rule and order. We act as trustees with ragard to material possessions committed to our charge. If the greed for worldly goods and acquisition could be neutralized, we could do away with war and all other attendant evils. The personality of an individual counts, above all tradition and customs.

Will it be too much to expect that the religions represented here will extend towards each other the same spirit of mutual respect and tolerance that Jesus evinced towards those of other religions, and thereby help us to usher in the annunciation to the shepherds, "Glory to God in the Highest, on earth Peace, Goodwill towards men"?

APPENDIX

CHURCH AND CIVIL DISOBEDIENCE

(Being the correspondence between the Most Rev. Dr. F. Westcott, Lord Bishop of Calcutta and Metropolitan of India, and J. C. Kumarappa during April and May 1930.)

PREFATORY NOTE

The civil disobedience movement of 1930 was started by Gandhiji's March to Dandi and the Salt Satyagraha. The Government in its attempt to suppress it used all manner of means which were objectionable. The following appeal was sent to Christian Missionaries with personal letters to a few church dignitaries. This led to the correspondence with the Most Rev. F. Westcott, Lord Bishop of Calcutta, and Metropolitan of India, which was published in part, in some of the Diocesan Magazines and other journals, and in full in *Young India*, of June 26th 1930, and which is now here reprinted.

Maganwadi, Wardha,

J. C. KUMARAPPA.

An Appeal to all Christian Workers and Missionaries

Dear Friends,

We are at present passing through one of the greatest crises in India's long history, a crisis that bids fair to leave its mark not only on India but on humanity itself. The days when personal differences were fought out by duels is practically a thing of the past. Private individuals no longer appeal to brute force. But nations are still resorting to barbarous methods of violence; and might is right in international disputes. There has been a race for armaments in spite of repeated efforts at reducing them since the World War. There is no need for me to point out, at this late hour, that warfare reduces us to the level of brutes, and mechanized warfare o one even below that. We need to exert ourselves to rise to, at least, a human level, if not to a spiritual plane. Enlightened men the world over have been striving for what William James calls "a moral equivalent for warfare", as a means of settling national disputes. Before our very eyes Gandhiji is substituting for warfare the gospel of love in a practical way.

The details may have to be worked out to a great degree of refinement before Satyagraha can be used on an universal scale, but the basic principle is the one that concerns us vitally at this moment.

What is going to be the contribution of those of us who profess to follow the Prince of Peace whose banner is love? At this juncture a great responsibility is laid on our shoulders which we dare not shirk. Here is an opportunity at our very door the like of which christendom has never faced before. Do we not hear the Man of Sorrows say "He that taketh not his cross and followeth after me is not worthy of me"? The choice is imminent.

I am perfectly aware that our political views may honestly differ and we may be poles apart. Amongst christians, there are Indians and foreigners, and those who see eye to eye with the national movement, and those who may honestly believe that the Nationalists are misled. But there can be no difference of opinion regarding non-violence amongst those who were enjoined by their Master "Whosoever shall smite thee on the right cheek, turn to him the other also", and to return good for evil.

No appeal is necessary to those who are in full agreement with Gandhiji, and who are convinced that this movement is to clothe the naked and feed the hungry, as these friends are committed to non-violence.

My appeal is mainly to those who differ from the national cause. They have a great function to perform. I know some of the foreign Missionary friends are here under a contract with the British Government not to interfere in politics. But where non-interference means compromising a principle which they hold fundamental, I submit that they are bound in loyalty to their Lord to impress upon their Government the duty of adopting non-violent methods, even at the risk of their very lives. I am quite conscious that their's is a more difficult task than swimming with the current of the national movement but I am certain that the greater task offers a greater opportunity to "let your light so shine before men that they may see your good works and glorify your Father which is in heaven".

In to-day's issue of *Young India* there are cited numerous cases of brutalities practised by the police. I give here the following two reports only:

From Delhi:

"The volunteers were wounded as the police tried to wrest from our hands a bucket of salt. Only after they had belaboured us to their hearts' content could they dispossess us of our salt . . . . Among the wounded the five were seriously injured. They had been heavily belaboured on the chest and the abdomen. Two received severe injuries on their private parts."

From Dholera :

"Eight to ten policemen fell upon Ambalal. They brutally pressed his testicles struck him with fists on the chest and abdomen, pressed their fingernails on his neck, so much so that Ambalal fell senseless. Mr. . . . . and others quietly witnessed the brutality."

After these accounts no more words from me will be needed to commend to your Christian spirit the noble cause of non-violence. As far as the Satyagrahis themselves are concerned they pride in their tribulations and thank God for the opportunity of suffering much for what they hold to be a righteous and sacred cause like the early Christian martyrs. But that does not condone the violence on the Government's side. I am confident that no true Christian, be he Indian or foreign, will leave a stone unturned in finding ways and means of persuading the Government to use human methods in their attempt to "maintain law and order".

17th April, 1930.

Yours sincerely,
JOSEPH CORNELIUS KUMARAPPA

19th April, 1930

Most Rev. Dr. F. Westcott,
Lord Bishop of Calcutta and
Metropolitan of India, Calcutta.

Dear Dr. Westcott,

Yesterday I posted to you a copy of my appeal to Christians and Missionary bodies. I am enclosing another for ready reference.

It seems a terrible reflection that a Government responsible to a nation that supports the Christian Church as a national institution should perpetuate such atrocities and especially on non-Christians. This will do incalculable damage to the cause of the Christian Church in India. If the Church does not register its protest — and that right early — and urge the Government to at least follow the lead in non-violence given by Gandhiji, great service may be rendered even by getting resolutions passed by the various Christian organizations and forwarding copies of these to the Government and to the press.

May I respectfully point out that with Christians non-violence cannot be treated as a matter of policy. It is one of the basic principles inculcated and practised by Christ. If this be so then it is incumbent upon the Church, I submit, to undertake to propagate the principle of non-violence. Should not something constructive be done to organize a permanent movement having for its object the promotion of non-violent methods of settling disputes? I am addressing Bishop Fisher and others on this subject but as nothing can give this movement a greater impetus than a definite lead from you I trust this matter will receive your prayerful consideration and then I am persuaded you will see your way made clear to undertake this responsibility.

I remain,
Yours sincerely,
J. C. KUMARAPPA

Bishops' House, Calcutta.
24th April, 1930.

My Dear Sir,

I received your letter of the 19th inst. and no doubt you write to me as one who has known Mahatma Gandhi for some years and who deeply appreciated the service he was rendering for the social uplift of the depressed classes and for racial unity in India. As a social reformer, he had my whole hearted support, for in doing that he seemed to me to be truly following in the footsteps of Jesus Christ, but now you ask me to support him when he has, unlike Jesus Christ, identified himself with the political aspirations of the Nationalists. You will remember the multitudes sought Jesus Christ to make Him their King that He might lead them to assert their national independence and secure their freedom from Roman Rule. This He absolutely refused to do regarding it as a temptation of the devil to be resisted.

You seem to assert that our Lord would have approved civil disobedience and would have called upon Governments when any of their subjects deliberately violated the laws of the country to go on and break others with impunity. It is hard to understand how you could imagine that this is God's way of ordering His world. When I look to nature, I find that what we call "Natural Law" is absolutely fixed and reliable. On that fixity of law depends our power of carrying on our daily work and the research students depend upon it for making further discoveries. I remember well Father Wagget saying to a great meeting in the Albert Hall, "that if butter was sometimes as hard as iron and iron was sometimes as soft as butter at the same temperature, we could make neither a bridge nor a breakfast." "Can we expect that Jesus Christ who came to reveal the character of God would so utterly repudiate this revelation of God given us in nature? We know he did not, for again He exhorted His disciples to obey the law. When the Pharisees wished to place Him in a dilemma, they asked him whether it was lawful to give tribute to Caesar or not and He asked them to show Him a current coin. They showed Him one with Caesar's likeness on it. His reply was, "Render unto Caesar the things that are Caesar's." You avail yourself of the safety which a stable Government affords you and of all the services which it provides for your convenience, but think you are at liberty to violate its laws with impunity. So far from encouraging any civil disobedience or religious disobedience, our Lord exhorted His disciples to obey the Scribes and Pharisees. He said, "Whatsoever they bid, that do and observe". Perhaps I need hardly remind you what St. Paul, a chosen witness of Jesus Christ wrote to the Romans.

> "Let every soul be in subjection to the higher powers; for there is no power but of God; and the power that be are ordained of God. Therefore he that resisteth the power, withstandeth the ordinance of God; and they that withstand shall receive to themselves judgment. For rulers are not a terror to the good work but to the evil."

Perhaps you recall our Lords injunction to the individual which forbade him to retaliate for a wrong done to him. Our Lord bade him to win over the evil doer by kindness and patience. He was not dealing at the time with the question of the maintenance of law and order in the State which finds its parallel in the natural order of the physical universe. A great deal of the suffering in the world is due to the violation of what we call " the

Laws of Nature". Much of such violation is done in ignorance but yet penalty of that violation is exacted. In the present civil disobedience, there is no question of ignorance. It is deliberate and is intended to over-throw the Government. I do not wish to discuss further the question of salt-tax or the excise policy of the Government. That is beside the point. What I am protesting against is that you should think the teaching or example of Jesus Christ gives any warrant for the practice of civil disobedience.

Yours faithfully,
Foss, Calcutta.

J. C. Kumarappa Esq., M. A. B. Sc.,
Gujarat Vidyapith,
Ahmedabad.

2nd May, 1930.

Most Rev. Dr. F. Westcott,
Lord Bishop of Calcutta and
Metropolitan for India, Calcutta.

Dear Bro. Westcott,

Thank you very much for your letter of the 24th April received yesterday. May I say how surprised I was to find you regaling me a homily on civil disobedience all through? I never even mentioned the words civil disobedience in my letter to you. What I wanted was not that you should suppport Gandhiji in his political campaign but that you should urge Government to use non-violent methods. Surely any Christian on either side can do that even while vehemently condemning the other side. I did not for a moment imagine that was too much to be expected of the head of the Anglican Church in India. At present the inhumane methods used by the Government towards the Satyagrahis is unworthy of an opponent like Gandhiji, and no gentleman can countenance it. leave alone one who professes to follow the Prince of Peace without a word of protest while such brutalities and tortures are being used. This attitude of callousness is tantamount to a denial of our Lord more culpable than that of Peter's and the only hope is that it may be followed by repentance and more ardent service as in the case of the rugged Apostle.

The next paragraph in my letter does not even refer to the present political situation but only to the application of the principle of non-violence in settling all manner of disputes. You have chosen to ignore this paragraph altogether. Perhaps you do not wish to follow Christ to the extent of non-violence. You will forgive me if I say that most of our missionaries and other leaders of the Christian Church seem to be Britishers first and Christians afterwards if convenient. You remember how during the World War practically every pulpit was turned into a recruiting sergeant's platform and every Church service ended with that morbidly narrow nationalistic song, "God save the King" which embodies the "tribal God" idea of King David. Christ's teachings are torn from the context and twisted passages are partially quoted to meet their national needs and the flocks committed to their charge are being misled. This is a grave charge which seems to apply even to you as I shall proceed to show presently. I do not know how far they are consciously guilty. They are themselves products of a civilization based on violence and so are not able to fully appreciate and interpret Christ's clear teaching on this subject. May God forgive them for the mischief they are doing, perhaps with the best of intentions, in this land which holds even plant life sacred. As an individual, I should have hesitated to approach the throne of the Metropolitan of

India, a prince among the prelates of the Church, in this fashion had it not been for the authority of the New Testament; and on this ground I would crave indulgence for anything that would have otherwise appeared presumptious in this letter. Since you have yourself raised the question of civil disobedience I have no option left but to deal with your arguments.

Emanating from such an exalted source the misapplication of scripture incidents and partial quotations contained in your letter in support of your own ideas came as a great shock to me. You refer to the multitude seeking to make Jesus King and you add "that he might lead them to assert their national independence and secure their freedom from Roman rule. This He absolutely refused to do regarding it as a temptation of the devil to be resisted". May I refer you to the actual context and passage John VI. 14 and 15 which follows on the description of the miracle of feeding of the five thousand men? "Then those men when they had seen the miracle that Jesus did said, this is of a truth that prophet that should come into the world. When Jesus therefore perceived that they would come and take him and make him a king, he departed again into a mountain himself alone."

The prophet they were expecting was the Messiah and the common conception was that he would be a temporal king and the context suggests clearly that these men were impelled by purely selfish motives—feeding the body. These people wholly misunderstood His mission and His kingdom which was not to be of this world and hence He departed. There is no mention or even room to infer all you say about national independence and freedom about Jesus regarding it as a temptation to be resisted. There is no idea of a temptation here at all.

Then later on you proceed to say "Our Lord exhorted his disciples to obey the Scribes and Pharisees". He said, "Whatsoever they bid that do and observe". In other words you allocate to the bureaucracy in India the same place in the political order that the Scribes and Pharisees of old held in the Jewish organization. I am absolutely one with you in this, but I resent your partial quotation calculated to misinterpret Jesus. You omit the first part of his injunction and fail even to refer to the later parts of the chapter. Matt. XXIII, Verse 2, says: "The Scribes and

Pharisees sit in Moses' seat" and then comes the third Verse: "All therefore whatsoever they bid that do and observe". That in so far as the Scribes and Pharisees are the custodians of Mosaic Law, which to the Jew was God-made Law or we may term a higher moral law. He wants them to obey this. But He never enjoins them to blind obedience as you will find right through the rest of the chapter one of the strongest condemnations of the Scribes 'and Pharisees' usurping the place rightfully due to the Mosaic or God-given Law and prostituting it to suit their own selfish ends and devouring widows' houses. Most of the Verses in this chapter begin with such biting words as "Woe unto you Scribes and Pharisees hypocrites", "Woe unto you ye blind guides", "Ye fools and blind" and ends up with "Ye serpents, ye generation of vipers, how can ye escape the damnation of hell". (And I say Amen to the bureaucrats of India). He has again and again exhorted them to "Beware of the Scribes and Pharisees". He never advocated blind obedience such as you imply. He enjoined them to follow the God-given Law. In Matt. V. repeatedly you have verses beginning with "Ye have heard that it was said by them of old time

. . . But I say unto you etc.", and in Verse 20, "Except your righteousness shall exceed the righteousness of the Scribes and Pharisees, ye shall in no case enter the Kingdom of Heaven". Surely if they were to follow meekly the Scribes and Pharisees they cannot excel them. He inculcated the pursuit of a higher moral law and said, "Fear not them that kill the body but are not able to kill the soul but rather fear Him which is able to destroy both soul and body in Hell." This is enough as far as His precept goes, but let us see what his practice was. Did he himself obey the Scribes and Pharisees in all things even where laws were immoral and anti-social? I need only refer you to the first few verses of Mark III where you will find a record of his civil disobedience against the Law of the Sabbath when he considered its operation anti-social. After spiritedly condemning it and the Scribes and Pharisees He defiantly broke it by healing the man with a withered hand. His action so enraged the then custodians of "Law and Order" that the Pharisees "Straightway took counsel with Herodias against Him, how they might destroy him". Sabbath was made for man and not man for the Sabbath. Wherever the man-made law has proved to be immoral, as in the case of the Salt Tax, and anti-social, as in the case of the excise policy, the righting process will lead to a disturbance of the peace. "Think not that I am come to send peace on earth. I came not to send peace but a sword." This is a solemn statement from the Prince of Peace. Do we not hear an echo of this last verse in Gandhiji's desire to present the Government of India with a string of broken heads? It is not the physical injury that matters but the fact that a broken head represents the zeal to do away with an immoral law. We hear a great ideal of criticism on this much misunderstood statement of Gandhiji.

You appear to have terribly confused the ideas of "Law of Nature" and man-made laws, and attribute the same potency and virtue to both alike. "Law" in Science is but the observed uniform order of sequence and hence the "fixity" you talk about is a fixity only until a variation from this uniformity is noticed, then even this "fixity" has to be modified. Therefore even in natural law there is nothing that is "absolutely reliable" as you so innocently imagine. Man-made laws are only rules laid down for the regulation of society and as no man is infalliable.— I am not sure what you think of the Pope—some of these regulations may be totally immoral or anti-social. Then what is our duty towards these? The example of Christ urges us to rise to that which is our highest light irrespective of consequences.

You accuse the people of taking advantage of the services of the Government. Are these services offered gratis? The way you speak of it one would imagine you were under that impression. Do you not realize even at this late hour that the very blood is squeezed out of the Indian peasant by way of taxes? Even if I grant, for argument's sake, that the service we get is desirable is there no idea of adequacy of payment? I am sure you will be the last one to justify the late war on the score that it called forth some heroism occasionally. Surely the price was too heavy to pay. This is one of the bases of contention of the Satyagrahis. According to you it would seem that the Goverment exists that the people might obey it. Man is made for the Sabbath theory. A most pernicious way to look at the relationship—you cannot get anywhere with such ideas. Instead of Government bending to the will of the people the bureaucracy says, "We will crush them down to accept our mandates". The Indian citizen — indeed if he can be called a citizen and not a slave — is made for maintaining a Government and finally the British trade.

The Scribes and Pharisees used the law to serve their own ends. Our present day Pharisees are not to be outdone in this. Take for instance "justice". This should be no respector of persons. Yet Gandhiji and innumerable other Satyagrahis are free while the Government picks and chooses whom they may devour. Law is at present the faithful handmaiden of the executive to carry out its will. Government is not there to maintain "Law and Order", but the Law is there to maintain the Government. Is this not an anti-social state of affairs?

To summaries the present movement in India, the Satyagrahis feel the anti-social nature of the whole system. Salt Tax, liquor sales etc., and realizing that at present man is made to be taxed, they are breaking such laws as are immoral (which question you conveniently refuse to discuss), not fearing them that can destroy the body by torture, machine guns and other accessories of "civilization", and the Pharisees — the bureaucrats — are taking counsel with Herodias — Whitehall — as to how they may destroy the greatest apostle of Christ to India. Not the kind that says, "Lord, Lord" but one that doeth the will of the Father is the same that Jesus owns to be his brother, sister and mother. You may ask how could I accuse Government of seeking to destroy him while he has been left unmolested. I have not seen Gandhiji since the campaign started, but I know the brutalities perpetrated on one of the least of the people will be an immeasurably greater torture to him than any that his hundred pounds of human flesh can be submitted to. The Satyagrahis follow Christ even to the court of the present day Pilates who rather than do justice and resign, stick to their posts and carry out the wishes of the powers that be. The Satyagrahis take no part in the proceedings even as Christ refrained. "Then said Pilate unto Him 'hearest thou not how many things they witness against thee?' and he answered him never a word in so much that the Governor marvelled greatly."

Western civilization brings formalities even between Christians. Formerly, I addressed you "Dear Dr. Westcott" and signed myself

'Yours sincerely' but you begin, 'My dear Sir and end 'Yours faithfully' but you will allow me to follow Matt. XXIII. 8 and address you 'Brother' and sign myself

Yours Fraternally,
J. C. Kumarappa.

II

AN OUTLINE OF A PLANNED ECONOMY

(This chapter has been culled from an article contributed to the Indian Journal of Social Work, March 1942. We are grateful to the Editorial Board of the Journal for permission to use this matter.)

In this part we shall attempt, with special reference to our own country, to obtain a bird's-eye-view of the general lines on which a Socio-Economic organization should strive to bring into practice the principles we had considered in Part I.

As Jesus says, "They that be whole need not a physician but they that be sick." The wealthy and the powerful are well able to take care of themselves, but only the general masses in our country, who are helpless and poverty-stricken need the attention of an organized society. Therefore, the trend of our approach will be directed towards that end.

True Democracy:— Democracy, as we find it in the West, is a delegated autocracy and differs little from the organization of totalitarian states. They are all in effect complete dictatorships, masquerading under variegated colourful names. The essence of democracy is that the executive and the legislative power must be vested in the people —in each individual. In an enlightened sense, each citizen must be capable of being a law unto himself. This endows him with the power to act not only rightly, but also wrongly. For such a state to work for the common good of all, a high standard of moral development in each citizen composing the state is an essential prerequisite. Everyone should be keenly conscious of his duties rather than his rights. The present so-called democracies are based on rights. An emphasis on rights leads to conflict ultimately. Insistence on rights is a primitive stage of evolution. Animals know no other relationship. But the more evolved man displays a keener sense of duties. Carrying out one's duties, even when irksome and against one's natural inclinations, call for a high order of self-discipline and self-control. When each citizen is so disciplined as to act on what is right, taking a detached view of affairs, he can be entrusted with the executive and legislative powers without fear of his misusing them. In such a state there is no placc for the army, navy, air force, or the police, as each citizen will act on the square, and his conscience will be his own policeman and legislature. Of course this is our final goal and will, when realized, be the Kingdom of Heaven on earth. At present we mortals are still imperfect and far from this state. Yet we have persons who are selfless and devoted to their ideals and seek their salvation in the service of their fellowmen. As a first step we shall accept society as it is. There are with us men who strive after following the economy of the cross, others who have reached the stage of gregarianism, and the majority are naturally in the economy of enterprise. Accordingly, we have to apportion the work of the nation. We may choose our delegates and repersentatives and ministers from the first group and gradually work up towards final stage.

Satyagraha : — The commonplace muddy politics are spiritualized by the use of. direct action through Satyagraha. By the use of this instrument to settle disputes one tries to win over one's opponent by persuasion, and failing that one invites suffering on oneself to draw out that which is highest in the opponent. In this method there is no room for the play of the baser elements of human nature. Anger, hatred and jealousy, often resulting even in murder, has been the order of the day in political life. But now an attempt should be made to appeal to the higher nature in man to settle differences amicably, rather than to might, violence, bloodshed, and the savagery of modern wars.

Government: — We have already pointed out that the aim of politics is to serve the masses. By political means we get control of Government and use Government functions to serve the needs of the people. In matters of State there are many things that call for a long view of affairs, which are naturally opposed to the short-sighted interests often governing the decisions of individuals. Therefore, such items have to be undertaken in the common interests of the nation, though in some cases these may be directly opposed to individual interests, have to be detailed out to a group of men who can be relied on to do their duty by the nation as a whole.

The members of this group, dedicated to the economy of Jesus, will not attempt to exploit their position; they will be paid an allowance not based on the fabulous profits made by merchants of rare ability, but on the earnings of the average citizen in the village. According to the Government Industrial Survey of the Central Provinces and Berar the average income of a villager is about a rupee per month. From the taxes drawn from such persons it would be iniquitous to pay thousands a month to those who are supposed to serve him. The best of village industries cannot pay more than about Rs. 75/- per month per family. Hence, even a salary of Rs. 200/- per month for the Commissioner of a Division would be on the liberal side. That being so, all other emoluments will be scaled down accordingly. The fees of lawyers, doctors, etc., and the remuneration of engineers, teachers and other public servants, will also fall in line. At present the princely salaries of Government servants are setting a standard completely out of keeping with the country's capacity to pay. It is this anomalous standard that is responsible for driving all the educated into clerical jobs. If we would have the educated take interest in the villages, we have to alter this glamorous attraction of the desk. The Government being the largest single employer and spender, it has the responsibility of directing employment to desired channels by its planned expenditures. Our National Government has to take this into account. The Congress Government made a good beginning by limiting the highest salaries to Rs. 500/. The full implication of this step is not often realized. It has far reaching consequences.

Functions:—Apart from efficient administration, the Government has to play the important role of the chief partner in the business of the people. The economic activities of the nation can be controlled, for better or for worse, by the organization of Forests, Minerals, Power Resources, and Communications. These governmental functions will, of course, be based on the principles that belong to the economy of permanence.

Forests:—The forests represent the perennial stream from which the people will draw their raw materials for their industries. Our country is rich in forest wealth but it is not planned so as to supply the materials as and when the people need them. When a carpenter needs wood, he buys what he can in the market. Such wood is not seasoned, so the article he makes cracks or warps. Seasoning wood takes time and no carpenter can afford the capital to stock logs long enough to season, nor would he have the space. It therefore, falls to the lot of the Forest Department to season the wood in the forests before unloading it on the market. Similarly, there are a thousand and one articles from the forest which can be controlled and regulated to supply the needs of the people and keep up the level of their economic activity. This aspect of forest management is more or less ignored today. That which weighs with the government is the revenue yielding capacity of forests.

Minerals:—Mines and quarries form the treasure trove of the people. Unlike the forests, these are likely to be exhausted by exploitation. Hence, great care must be taken to make the best use of them. They represent potential employment for the people. When ores are sent out of the country, the heritage of the people of the land is being sold out. It is the birthright of the people to work on the ores and produce finished articles. Today, in India most of the ores are being exported. We are, therefore, not only losing the opportunities of employment for the people but impoverishing the land. Minerals, like other rawmaterials, have to be worked into consumable articles and only after that can the commerce part of the transaction commence. Any government that countenances a foreign trade in the raw materials of a country is doing a disservice to the land. A Swaraj Government will not only organize the exploitation of the raw materials for the people, but will help them to use these in their industries. Here is the rightful place for large scale industries under the control of the Government. A steel plant may produce steel bars and plates, but not buckets and ploughs. The latter should be the preserve of the village blacksmith.

Power:—Supply of cheap power and light can be undertaken by Government by harnessing the water power in the land. This, too, has to be directly under Government control, if not Government-owned.

Communication:—Roads, canals, railways, shipping, and the like, have to be provided by the Government. Apart from the paucity of canals, the railways have had a monopoly of transport for long distances. The flow of goods has been controlled by carefully scheduled, discriminating, special rates. This must be done in the interests of the people. Today such railways as we have, have helped to drain raw materials from the land, and to bring foreign manufactures into the remotest villages. This policy has been one that has brought about the ruin of industry in India, in no small measure. To give only one instance in connection with the oil-pressing industry, which is one of the large industries of India: If one takes 100 maunds of Mohua seeds to Bombay from C. P., it costs Rs. 46-6-0; but if the oil is pressed at Akola, C. P., and the oil and cake from 100 maunds of Mohua seeds are transported to Bomby, it costs Rs. 77-15-0. This means that the oil press in C P. has a handicap of Rs. 31-9-0 per 100 maunds on the freight alone, and that the tendency of the seed, therefore, is to go to Bombay. There are over ten thousand such special rates. A National Government will undo this injustice at the first possible moment, and control the the traffic in the interests of the villagers' economic activity. The railway may be a good instrument but can also be used effectively to impoverish the people by depriving them of employment. It is a double edged sword.

Taxation:—To carry out their work the Government has to find the wherewithal.

This comes from taxation. We have to be careful to see that the incidence of taxation does not fall unduly heavily on the taxpayer who is below the subsistence level. When the taxes are collected, the expenditures of Government should be so made as to increase the taxable capacity of the citizen. When the taxes are gathered from the villages, and expenses which benefit the towns are met out of them, impoverishment of the people results. We have already seen one safeguard in the scale of salaries; another important safety valve is in the collection of taxes in kind. However inconvenient it may be to gather taxes in kind, such an exchange prevents marginal loss in the national income. The allowances to officials can be met partly in kind. This old system still prevails in most of the Muslim countries. In the Pathan states of the N. W. F. P., it is working well to this day.

Expenditures :—When taxes are received from one area and much of it is spent in another, impoverishment of the former takes place. If money received from the farmers is spent on buildings in New Delhi, the country is the poorer for it. As far as possible taxmoneys must be spent as near the place of collection as possible. Cheapness of a foreign article may be a consideration for a private citizen but not to the Government. If the Government spends tax money for paper from Sweden, it is against the interests of the taxpayer, if paper made locally can be obtained. If the Government pays one anna for foreign paper, and the local paper can be had for one and a half annas even this higher price is more economical from the country's point of view. In the first case one anna goes out of the country; a local purchase, on the other hand, gives employment to the taxpayer and keeps the money in circulation. Hence, all Government expenditures must as far as possible be spent within the "catchment-area" of taxation.

Large Scale Industries :—By their very nature and organization, large scale industries control the lives of many individuals. In a true democracy no private citizen should have this power. Therefore, all large scale industries must be State owned and State managed.

Most such industries cannot run without various forms of help from the Government. We have already mentioned discriminations in freight rates. For large-scale productions various conveniences, such as ports, quays, docks and railways, are needed. When these are provided at the expense of the taxpayers such benefit, if extended to private concerns, becomes a subsidy out of public moneys to concerns run for private profit. This cannot be allowed. Tax money must be spent for the general benefit. From this point of view also all such large-scale industries must be run by the State.

Large scale industries are needed in exploiting natural resources which should form the raw materials of the peoples' industries. Control of such raw materials cannot be left in private hands. Therefore, all such industries should also be under the State.

In economics large scale industry, is the antithesis of democracy in politics. It is not by chance that the Western nations have come by their economic organization. It is a result of their way of thinking in terms of autocracy. They find themselves with dictatorships in political organization, and centralized industries in the economic field. These two go together and we cannot have the one without the other.

If we aim at true democracy, we have to abandon centralized production in consumption goods. This does not preclude all centralized industries. As we have already seen, there is a definite field for such, though restricted. Within these limits of Government controlled and owned industries, supplying raw materials to the people, providing public utilities and manufacturing instruments, etc., there is a large field of work for such units. Just as certain chemicals used in minute quantities may prove to be healing portions, and when used in large doses may prove fatal poisons, so also centralized units can be a blessing to the people when properly coordinated with the people's economic activities and not used for the exploitation of the masses. This can only be done when such industries are run on a service basis even at a loss. Therefore, their natural place is only as a part of the Government organization of the country, acting on the principles that govern an economy of Gregarianism.

ECONOMIC ACTIVITY OF THE PEOPLE

People should have freedom to occupy themselves in supplying their own demands. How this can be planned is simple. Restricted profit motive is a good regulator of industries. The problem before the world today is not one of production but one of distribution. Hence any method we decide on has to be a good distributor.

Distribution :—The wealth of a nation consists not in what a few possess, but in the extent to which the great majority can satisfy their daily wants, especially needs. Looked at from this angle, increase in the number of millionaires in a country need not indicate increase in the prosperity of the nation. Indeed, it may indicate the opposite, if the accumulated wealth has been occasioned by restricted distribution. Then judging the well-being of a nation, our consideration should centre upon the way in which purchasing power is distributed among the citizens. If we adopt this criterion, then industries which distribute wealth are better for the masses than industries that help a few to accumulate a great store of riches. This means that mills, which being centralized assist in accumulating wealth, are detrimental to the interests of the masses; and cottage indusries, which distribute wealth, are by far the better method to adopt, especially in our country, where we are faced with a shortage, not of labour, but of capital. Therefore, the method of economic organization we choose must be one which takes this factor into consideration.

The centralized methods of production accumulate wealth and power in the hands of a few, and require a considerable amount of accumulated capital to start with. This last factor removes such methods from within the reach of the masses, and does not fulfil our requirements as a distributor. Capitalistic systems, and centralization, are based on the presumption of capital being available. In our country where such accumulated wealth is scarce, and poverty is widespread, we have to found our organization on revenue. That means that the whole system must depend for its efficient working on the day-to-day labour of the people. A palace built with highly skilled labour has to be repaired and kept in order by skilled labour, but a hut built with mud can be kept clean by the inhabitants themselves, with their own labour. The former presumes availability of capital but the latter is based on the availability of labour.

Division of labour :— The work a person is engaged in, and the daily duties he performs, must be such as to contribute to the fullest development of his personality. Sub-divison of processes, which is necessary for standardized production under centralized methods, provides no scope for originality, nor for the play of initiative. The worker in a centralized industry becomes a mere cogwheel of the huge machine.

He loses his individuality and freedom of action.

The people of our land are extremely poor. Labour is plentiful, but capital is scarce. A non-violent society striving after the economy of Jesus must therefore be based on revenue and not on capital. These considerations lead us to advocate methods of production which involve little or no capital, and for which raw materials and a ready local market for findished products are easily available. However much we may desire it otherwise, we cannot change these factors, and any planning which ignores these will not succeed. Therefore, we are logically driven to the position which envisages village industries as the central occupation of the people. For these and other reasons that we have cited earlier, under "Large Scale Industries," we cannot recommend the centralized methods of production for the masses.

Thus the general economic activity of the masses will follow the principles of the economy of Enterprise, within limits set by the Government operating on the economy of Permanence, as has been indicated above. In no case will the economy of Predation be tolerated as between man and man.

Ahimsak Swadeshi :— True Swadeshi seeks to discharge the responsibilities of a consumer or buyer as a trustee. A business transaction does not begin and end with the transfer of goods and payment of money; in addition, it involves the consideration of one's duties to one's fellow-men. One who buys an article takes it with all the moral values attached to the goods. If one buys a stolen article one becomes party to that offence. This is the responsibility and trusteeship of wealth. So it is the duty of every consumer to know the conditions under which things he needs are produced. If he patronises goods made under objectionable conditions, he becomes a party to it.

Centralization is nothing and decentralization is nothing, if we have not the love that binds man and man. We are often told that Japan uses the cottage method largely. We have to see if the final effect is for the good of all people. If Japan uses the cottage method to exploit China, we can no more tolerate that than centralized industries. A few months ago Gandhiji issued a warning to the public not to buy Khadi from uncertified dealers. What is the difference ? Materially there is no differnce, but viewed from the moral and humane standpoint there is a world of difference. The Charkha Sangh insists on a subsistence wage being paid to the producers. Therefore, the Charkha Sangh Khadi is honest cloth, bearing its cost, while the other may be the result of exploitation and hence may be said to include human misery in its composition. Hence, we must beware of even decentralized industries. One who wants to be sure of the moral purity of an article should buy articles manufactured under his range of knowledge. If it is not possible for us to guarantee the conditions under which articles are manufactured in distant lands we should restrict our patronage to our neighbourhood. This is Ahimsak Swadeshi.

Political Swadeshi may mean goods produced within certain political or geographical boundaries. In this there may be no need for moral values and it may lead to hatred when foreign goods are boycotted from such considerations. Refraining from buying goods which are not manufactured by one's neighbours carries no such harted, but is a sign of one's own limitations. The political boycott may lead to war but true Swadeshi will knit neighbours together.

Costs :—A great part of the money spent on cottage-made articles goes towards payment of wages. The materials themselves cost very little, but in mill-made articles, while the least expense is on labour, the bulk is for overhead charges, sales organization, and materials. The economics of Western manufacturers are dictated by low prices, but for the prosperity of an agricultural people, high prices composed largely of human labour are welcome. High prices of cottage industry products also help in the distribution of wealth which means it contributes largely to the welfare of the people.

Self-help :—The capitalistic system depends for its development on the helplessness of its customers. The more helpless the customer the more sure it is of its markets. It seeks to kill all initiative in the customer. Indeed, the capitalistic strúcture is raised on a foundation of the tombstones of consumers' initiative. In cottage industries the principle desideratum is the consumer's initiative; we expect every one to be resourceful.

Every person, whether interested in the production of an article or in its consumption, should be aware of the possibilities in village industries. Life is one whole. Division of labour there must be, but dissection and division of processes leads to unmitigated drudgery. Proper work, when intelligently carried out, is an aid to culture. It brings out all that is best in an individual, and helps to develop his faculties.

Conclusion :— Within the limited space at our disposal it has not been possible to give a full life-size picture of planned activities, but we have just introduced the subject to show how we are to obtain freedom for every individual, and use political power to harness Government functions towards the improvement of the economic condition of the people by the supply of good raw materials, and tools, and by the dissemination of scientific information. The people in their turn occupy themselves in industries of their own without exploiting their neighbours. Such contacts as we have with sister nations, will be cultural and commercial, as in the past, and will not be through political domination.

In short, we may state that an economy of Permanence may be inaugurated by the following steps :

1. The general policies of the Government being moulded in accordance with the principles of the economy of Permanence.

2. The permanent government servants being recruited from persons who have dedicated their lives to the economy of the Cross. Government experts may have to be drawn from the general masses, following the economy of enterprise.

3. The organization and administration of public utilities and services, and centralized and large scale industries, will be based on the economy of Gragarianism.

4. The general masses will carry on their economic activities under the economy of Enterprise, within the scope indicated and controlled by the Government.

It is only through such means that we can all dwell in peace under an economy of Permanence. It may not be possible for us to maintain such a high artificially created standard of living as some classes in the Western nations have attempted to do, but we shall be able to obtain all the natural needs, the comforts and even luxuries necessary for us, without living on the oppression of those who happen to be weaker than us. This is the only way to obtain peace and good will among men. These methods may not appeal to some of us, who have imbibed the Western modes of thoght and action but we have to think out fully the consequences of all other ways suggested. If such alternatives as may be thought of fail to achieve our objective, and the present debacle in Europe has conclusively proved the impotency of Capitalism, Fascism, Nazism and Communism to bring man out of his primitive barbarism and blood-thirsty savagery, we shall have no other course left. If we take to this programme, India will have the proud privilege of giving the lead to humanity at large, to live together amicably in the mutual enjoyment of peace, contentment and prosperity, ushering in the Kingdom of Heaven according to the will of God, and confering on man the dignity of a Son of God.